COUVADE

COUVADE

A Dream-Play of Guyana

Michael Gilkes

Introduction by Wilson Harris

Dangaroo  Press

COUVADE

First published 1974 by Longman Group Limited.

Cover Painting by Aubrey Williams

© Michael Gilkes

This edition published by
Dangaroo Press in 1990
Australia: Box 1209 GPO Sydney, NSW 2001
Denmark: 'Pinds Hus', Geding Søvej 21,
         8381 Mundelstrup, Denmark
U.K.: P.O. Box 186, Coventry CV4 7HG

ISBN 1 871049 70 9

For Joan

Contents

	Page
Note on the ritual of 'couvade'	vii
List of Characters	ix
Introduction	xi
Play	1

Note on the ritual of 'couvade' *by Michael Gilkes*

The *Penguin English Dictionary* carries the following entry:
'*Couvade* (kuvaad) n. (Fr.) custom among some primitive races in which a man takes to his bed while his wife is in childbirth.'

In fact a couvade is an extremely widespread ritual among so-called 'primitive races' like the Carib Indians where the father of the new-born child confines himself to his hammock, and must observe certain rules and taboos aimed at ensuring the child's health and happiness in the future. The 'civilised' equivalent of a couvade would seem to be the traditional chain-smoking or excessive drinking of the nervous father-to-be, and the self-congratulatory offering of cigars, if the child is a boy.

The 'primitive' version, however, usually entails personal hardship, voluntarily undertaken by the father. Among certain river-dwelling tribes, the custom, it is said, is to tie the father-to-be to a tree trunk below the high-water mark, during the final stages of his wife's labour. If the birth is delayed, his own life becomes (symbolically, if not actually) forfeit to the rising water. The father thus establishes a vital link with the unborn child.

The English anthropologist/explorer, Everard Im Thurn, published in 1883, his detailed account (*Among the Indians of Guiana* Kegan Paul, Trench) of the ritual of couvade as practised by the Carib Indians of Guyana: a ritual still observed by some tribes.

'Couvade is such a wide-spread institution, that I had often read and wondered at it. . . . It appears based on a belief in the existence of a mysterious connection between the child and its father – far closer than that which exists between the child and its mother, – and of such a nature that if the father infringes any of the rules of couvade, for a time after the birth of the child, the latter suffers.'

Richard Schomburgk, during his travels in Guiana in the 1840s, also observed the ritual of couvade among the Caribs. He observed one variant of couvade in which the man's ordeal of fasting was followed by a public ritual in which the man was cut all over the body with the teeth of an agouti. Blood from his wounds was then collected and rubbed on the child's skin. Schomburgk noted the symbolic nature of the ritual:

'that the child should inherit his courage, the father resigns himself, at the birth of his son or daughter, to (these) very painful ordeals.' (R. Schomburgk, *Travels in British Guiana* 1840–1844, Vol II, translated by Walter Roth, Georgetown, 1923).

List of Characters

(and the names of the actors who took part in the play's first performance at 'Carifesta', the first festival of Caribbean Arts, held in Guyana in 1972.)

Arawak Shaman	—	Carl Ngui-Yen
Pat	—	Rahana Karim/Mignon Lowe
Lionel/The Dreamer	—	Anthony Stewart
Mergency	—	Cedric Duncan
Santos	—	Ken Corsbie
Ashanti Priest	—	Alan Cooper/Lennox Foster
Eddie	—	Ken Corsbie
Arthur	—	Cedric Duncan
Pat's Father	—	Peter Bradford
Jordanite leader	—	Alan Cooper/Lennox Foster
The Nurse	—	Rahana Karim/Mignon Lowe

(Also attendants, dancers, workmen, Jordanite sisters.)

Translation of Black Carib Incantation
Idendéru túgúra búga
Dendé, dendé, dendé uamánia
Dendé, dendé, dendé uamitíha.

In the dream-time we had power
Power, power, let us again have power
Power, power, we will again have power.

An Approach to COUVADE *by Wilson Harris*

This is not intended as a conventional introduction but rather as a personal approach to a play I much admire.

A profound clue, it seems to me, to the expressive themes interwoven in COUVADE lies in the constellation of the Robe which assumes dramatic and terrifying proportions in the action of the play.

The Robe is an actual painting that Lionel, the artist-teacher, paints in his studio. That is obvious. The Robe is also part and parcel of the psychical text and texture of Lionel's dreams.

Lionel enters the Robe when it is uplifted by the Shaman and collapses on the stage. He gives "a hideous cry of anguish, his hands clawing at his face, pulling the thick paint down in streaks, like blood". (page 51)

Lionel's hallucinated dramatic entry into the Robe brings home consequences he has not bargained for. He is overwhelmed, it seems, by two forces or pressures upon him that we need to visualise as inwardly active in the drama of COUVADE. One force or pressure arises from the past (from absent ancestors to whom or which many allusions occur in the play) and it is as if the artist suffers the bite of ancestral furies as he falls to the ground. The other force or pressure comes from the unborn, from not-yet-present-being. As he collapses his pregnant wife, Pat, comes to his assistance and confirms her human and symbolic role as the embodiment of inner, future time. Thus non-being in the absent bodies of the ancestral past is threaded into a curious quantum value as it leaps or arches into futurity.

The pressures from past and future in a phenomenon of dramatic presence is at the heart of the Robe. Through such pressures we may visualise, I would suggest, a tension between *community* (as the quantum link in the past and the future within presence or present moment) and *individualism* in its narrow and circumscribed basis in the society to which Lionel belongs.

It is a bitter tension that is wonderfully manifest in the 'surreal' (so to speak) and the 'real' (so to speak) apparatus of the play as though the intellectual temper of a collective individualism - however concerned with the ills of society - resists the leap of transfigurative community gestating in consciousness and unconsciousness. Lionel's collapse therefore would appear to be inevitable as it highlights the core of barren resistance to profoundest creativity in his civilisation at large.

The individual artist, the individual teacher, the individual politician, and so on, are all agents of complex inner/outer tradition - however varied in talent or gift one or the other may be - and without a shared comprehension of the bite of creative conscience (and how this may be transformed or translated into the lived life) the individual person, all alone, suffers the blow of visionary truth. Such is Lionel's tragedy as the play progresses.

Yet it would be wrong to visit total tragedy upon him and upon the art of the play. At another level COUVADE is an evocation of peculiar, however, overshadowed, hope: hope that is in a state of gestation within the body of unrealised but not unrealisable community.

In this light which illumines the action of the play Lionel's failure - and the blindness of his colleagues who perceive his collapse as a mental breakdown pure and simple - may be grasped as the source of dramatic and imaginative strength in the context of the play to repudiate facile models of ascendancy. Lionel is not a facile, victorious teacher or a facile, victorious artist in ascendancy over his society. For such victory or success would have been forged by techniques of sublimation in the hollow refinement of the pressures to which he has been subject. Whereas his intuitive quest - in collaboration with various masks that the shaman wears, in collaboration with potent configurations of dream and reality in the movement of the play - is towards the exposure of a connecting door between genuine change and the destructive element that despairs of, even as it may subconsciously desire, genuine change in society or a new genesis and birth of the imagination. That destructive element - which we see for instance at a political meeting that takes place at a street corner where violence erupts and a stone is thrown - is so shot through by numinous substance in the action of the play that it is in essence the *energy* of a creative cosmos or mind in a state of disorientation that inclines it to the ritualisation of disaster.

The implicit connecting door in the architecture of the play between genuine capacity for change and destructive power or disorientation of the creative mind is so alarming - so outside of conventional expectation or criteria - that it brings Lionel down, it appears to break him, but what is clear is that the mere sublimation of violence into a refined artefact would have been for him an empty victory.

Through the connecting door in the symbolic architecture of the play we may visualise Lionel's crucial situation as an artist in correspondence with the political debate that takes place in the street when a stone is flung and one of the participants in the political meeting is badly injured. The flung stone runs in parallel with a thrown book that strikes Lionel's pregnant wife Pat in the stomach. The book is inadvertently flung across the studio by Arthur, Lionel's friend, who is exasperated by the painter's obsessions. Pat may have suffered a miscarriage. I mention this because the parallel endorses, I think, the disorientation to which I referred earlier. The book in the artist's studio is a vessel of scholarship and learning. It suffers peculiar dream-conversion, as it were, into an object that strikes and potentially maims. That Pat suffers the blow and recovers in an omen of the resources of mental/physical energy to save or destroy.

If violence is absolute then learning and art are an ultimate miscarriage and hollow. Whereas if a connecting door runs between creative hope and the terror of destructive order then hollowness becomes a new vessel, a new vibration. Hollowness is susceptible to *unstructured mediation* between all partial images, masks, characterisations, all partial manifestations within the body or bodies of COUVADE. The movement of the play towards harmony or a vessel of wholeness is necessarily overshadowed by what appears to be the nemesis of barren individualism. Except that that nemesis or hollow is pregnant with a passage from non-being into futurity.

Michael Gilkes's COUVADE is one of the most significant plays to have come out of the twentieth century Caribbean.

June 1988

Part One

The Sleepers

Scene One

On a totally darkened stage lights come up to reveal a small clearing in the Guyana rainforest. Filtering down through the (invisible) upper storey of the trees – giant greenheart, mora, etc. the dappled moonlight picks out an Amerindian benab in which (there are no walls) a hammock is slung, its occupant asleep as in a cocoon or canoe of darkness. Background noises: the sound of tree frog, cicada, the occasional cry of a goatsucker ('who you?') fade in and hold for about 20 seconds. Music comes up as background noises gradually fade. Very faintly, but growing gradually louder as it approaches, the music is a weird mixture of gourd, flute, deep braying of bamboo horn, drum; the discordant but clear bone flute melody rising above a gentle, slow, but definite rhythm. An oddly attractive, ethereal yet barbaric sound.

The figures of a SHAMAN *and his* TWO ATTENDANTS *approach. The* SHAMAN *takes up a squatting position c.s. which is slowly flooded in a faint pool of light. The* TWO ATTENDANTS *sit quietly in the background while the* SHAMAN *speaks. An incredibly old man, he is frail as ash; his skin pouched and wrinkled, papery-thin like a spider's or a lizard's. His voice is at once tired and authoritative, suggesting power as well as suffering. It has a curiously alien sound partly because of its unusual guttural placing of vowels, its peculiar stress and pace.*

SHAMAN	Every night we come here where Couvade sleeps
	out of the eye of Wiyeyu
	We come to ask Makanater
	Great Earthmaker
	To hear the dream of Couvade.
	Idendéru túgura búga
ALL	Dendé dendé dendé uamitíha
	Dendé dendé dendé uamánia

1

SHAMAN I make the bird of ash: Guacháro [*Sprinkles dust*]
I make the bird of water: Tukúiu [*Sprinkles water from small gourd*]
Let the bone flute speak [*Raises rattle*]

ALL Dendé dendé dendé uamánia
Dendé dendé dendé uamánia

SHAMAN Hear, O Makanater
Your children ask you
To receive these offerings:
Guacháro, Tukúiu
This milk of the calabash
This small bit of manioc
Milk of the land
Which comes from our heart.
We speak
From our heart.
For this we are stooping low
Beside you
Before you
Beneath you.
Receive them great Earthmaker
Receive us, Lord of the Forest
So that we may walk
In your eye.
So that we may walk
In your heart.

ALL Dendé dendé dendé uamánia
Dendé dendé dendé uamánia.

SHAMAN [*Gestures towards hammock*]
Sleep Couvade
Dream your dream
When you awake
Forest will die
Deer tiger tapir howler-monkey
Die
Fishes will die
Tukúiu, Guacháro will fly away
Behind the cloud.
Our people die.

Canoe of Makanater
Will not sail across the sky.
Sleep Couvade
And dream our dream.
[*Suddenly emphatic*] Itúke Makuári – ué:

ATTENDANTS [*Loudly*] Itúke Makuári – ué:

ALL Bínari tánura mánore ímu
Dendé dendé dendé uamánia
Dendé dendé dendé uamánia

Scene Two

As the music fades and lights dim, SHAMAN *and* ATTENDANTS *slowly leave. Rainforest scene is struck* [*the benab, 'trees', etc, are removed, leaving the hammock, which is a 'permanent' fixture*] *and quickly converted into* LIONEL'S STUDIO *with paintings on wall, table, armchair c.s. easel, books, sculpture, etc. An untidy room, containing the debris of last night's 'session'. Empty glasses, bottles are everywhere. The figure still asleep in hammock. The lights come up gradually, and the area outside the window gets brighter and brighter as the sun rises. A cock crows. It is morning.*
PAT *enters s.r. She is visibly pregnant, thirtyish, a dark Indian/African mixture and a small person attractive rather than good-looking. She looks at the sleeping figure in the hammock then at the general disorder of the room and starts clearing up the odd bottles, glasses, etc. The sleeper stirs.*

PAT Lionel? [*Goes up to him*] Li? [*He groans*] You not getting up this morning?

LIONEL Unh . . . ? What time is it?

PAT [*Busying herself with the clearing-up*] Half-past nine. [*An exaggeratedly agonised groan from the hammock. A leg appears dangling over the side.*] Well, you-all had a real session last night.

LIONEL [*Half-rising, his hand over his eyes*] Shades, love. Pass them for me. Over there by the table. [*She gives them to him and he puts them on, sitting cross-legged in the hammock.*]

PAT   [*Matter of factly, still busy with the clearing-up*] How
                it ended up this time? I heard you-all arguing down
                here till must be about one o'clock this morning.
                [*Silence from the hammock. A pause*] I don't know how
                you can get any sleep in that hammock. [*Pause. He
                seems to have fallen asleep sitting.*] What time they left?

LIONEL   [*Lies back in hammock and pulls sides of it over his body
                so that he is totally encased, enclosed in it*] Half past two.

PAT   Look, next time you-all try and have your get-together
                at one of the others' houses.

LIONEL   [*Speaking through the hammock*] Last week we met at
                Arthur's place, remember?

PAT   Why you don't have these meetings at the school?

LIONEL   [*Still wrapped in the hammock*] And have the old boy
                snooping around? He might hear something about his
                precious school he mightn't like.

PAT   So you prefer to meet and talk behind the poor man's
                back?

LIONEL   [*Rising from the depths of the hammock, only his head
                showing*] Behind the poor... Look. If that old fool
                were to hear the truth about himself – just a tiny bit of
                the truth – it would kill him. We would all be
                murderers. Besides he is not a poor man and anyway
                we have better things to talk about. [*Drops down in
                hammock again*]

PAT   [*Sarcastic*] Art and Politics, I suppose. Hm. It must
                have been a really important meeting last night,
                judging from all the empties. Your intellectual friends
                like they always thirsty.

LIONEL   [*From within the hammock, wearily*] It's Sunday, Pat.
                For Christ's sake don't start ...

PAT   I'm not starting anything. [*A pause*] Just look at this
                mess!

LIONEL   [*He gets out of hammock. He is in shorts only. His clothes are thrown over the armchair c.s. and on to the floor.*] Leave it. I'll clear it up. [*She picks up his vest from the floor.*] I said I'll do it. [*Takes it from her*]

PAT   O.K. O.K. I heard you. [*Sits in armchair c.s. As he dresses she watches him with a wife's indulgent look of intimacy and casual possessiveness, automatically handing him things – a sock, shirt, etc.*] You're not doing yourself any good by wearing those things in the house, you know. Lionel, why you don't go to the doctor about your eyes? You wear those shades far too much to do your eyes any good.

LIONEL   Look, it's just eyestrain [*Pulls on shirt*]. My eyes hurt because I've been working too hard, reading too much . . .

PAT   . . . and drinking too much. [*Picking up a bottle from under chair and holding it out accusingly*]

LIONEL   [*Taking the bottle and putting it on the table*] Drinking doesn't give you eyestrain. See my sandals anywhere? [*Drops down on knees to look under table*]

PAT   [*Points to a piece of driftwood sculpture: the sandals are stuck on its jutting ends*] Look up there. On your Tacouba Sculpture. Funny place to keep them.

LIONEL   [*Sucks teeth*] I bet Eddie put them there [*Reaches up, takes them off.*] That's your brother's idea of a joke. [*She laughs*] No respect for art.

PAT   Oh, he respects it all right. He just doesn't take it as seriously as you.

LIONEL   Eddie? He doesn't take ANYTHING seriously.

PAT   [*Looking at him with a smile*] No. Not even himself.

LIONEL   He and Arthur said they were coming round after lunch today. I want Arthur to see this new painting – you remember. The one I started last week.

PAT   Yes. And you were like a bear with a sore head for days . . .

LIONEL	I finished it. Last night: after they left. [*Goes towards easel, turns it round and brings it forward.*]
PAT	Lionel, you mean to say you stayed up painting after. . . ? Good Lord, you want to kill yourself or what? It's not enough that you're always working or reading or staying up late every night . . .
LIONEL	What do you think of it?
PAT	[*Looking at it embarrassed, not sure what is expected of her*] Hm! You're asking the right one. What are all those faces supposed to be?
LIONEL	Ancestral icons.
PAT	Ancestral who?
LIONEL	Icons. You know, like the carved figures on aboriginal totems. These [*He seems to be speaking to himself now*] these are Guyanese icons. Ancestral images that go back to our pre-Columbian past. [*She looks blank.*] Well? what do you think of it?
PAT	When Arthur comes you'll have to ask him. He's the art critic. Eddie and me could shake hands. I don't really understand all this intellectual business.
LIONEL	There's nothing intellectual about having an opinion, Pat. [*He carries on dressing*] If you don't like it all you have to say is you don't like it.
PAT	[*Hurt and on the defensive*] You don't really want my opinion. It's people like Arthur you want to impress.
LIONEL	[*Sits on chair putting on sandals. He pauses, looks at her*] You don't like Arthur, do you?
PAT	No.
LIONEL	Why?
PAT	I don't trust him.
LIONEL	Why not?

PAT   Because I don't. [*Sees his look of disgust at this piece of female logic*] Well, he's so puffed-up with himself! Always patting people on the back and when he's had a few drinks always ready to shout about 'power for the people' and 'black brotherhood' while all the time he's only thinking about himself. I'm sure his voice was the loudest down here last night.

LIONEL Pat . . .

PAT   He thinks he's the only one who's got any opinions at all.

LIONEL Pat, you're talking nonsense. Just because . . .

PAT   And I don't believe he respects you OR your work.

LIONEL [*Patiently and with some gentleness*] Look, love, just because he and I don't share the same point of view doesn't mean we don't respect each other. At least he's frank. He doesn't pretend to like my paintings. I respect him for it. A lot of our friends say they like my work, but they're not really interested. How many of them are prepared to BUY any of the paintings? Arthur's opinions are at least worth having.

PAT   The college is paying your salary. Why you have to bother so much with Arthur's opinions?

LIONEL Because he's an honest critic, love, and he does know something about art.

PAT   And I don't. At least I don't pretend to. But I DO know something about people . . .

LIONEL Here we go again . . .

PAT   You and he talk a lot about Art and Politics, but you don't seem to know much about real people. Sometimes I wonder if you yourself really understand all the fancy, high-sounding ideas you talk about. Politics is about people and it's people you paint for, isn't it? [*She goes over to the paintings.*] Look at this. Couvade. You and your Amerindian myths. Who would want to spend their money on that? And this. This latest one . . .

LIONEL [*Quietly, but with an edge to his voice*] Don't touch it. It's still wet.

PAT [*Sucks her teeth loudly*] I don't know. You're nearly as bad as Arthur. He with his talk about 'Mother Africa' and you with your Amerindian dreams. This is the sort of thing you're teaching your students?

LIONEL Oh no! [*His tone reveals a certain bitterness: the unpleasant but familiar pain of an old wound.*] No. We study the abstract beauty of tropical fruit in a bowl. We paint picturesque rural landscapes. You know, like Constable's *Hay Wain* but with a donkey cart instead. Some of the boys have been doing 'imaginative scenes from the hinterland'. Few of them have ever been further into the interior than Vreed-en-hoop or Diamond. Last Thursday the old boy announced that a prize would be given for the best painting by a student on the theme of the 1763 revolution. And guess what? They're all, it seems, doing portraits of Cuffy. Arthur would have approved. At least it's better than bowls of fruit. Christ, my head is splitting.

PAT [*She has not really understood all of this but is intuitively, practically, sympathetic. She has come up close, concerned, the good wife*] Li, you should eat something, you know. What about breakfast? You must be hungry.

LIONEL [*Seated, he puts his arms round her buttocks and pulls her in to him burying his face in her stomach. A gentle, intimate movement*] Mmmm . . . I'm always hungry. *You* know that.

PAT [*Her hands on his shoulders, she speaks in a softer, more intimate way. A kind of teasing sensuality that is at the same time quite unaffected*] I'm talking about breakfast. You know, you're getting as thin as a scarecrow. [*He pulls her down into his lap.*] Heyyy! CAREFUL, Li.

LIONEL [*Nuzzling her neck*] And YOU are getting as fat as a nice, juicy star-apple. [*Puts his hand on her stomach*] How's the baby behaving?

PAT   [*Kissing him*] Very well. Not like his wicked father.

LIONEL   [*Places his ear against her stomach*] You sure he's in there? [*Raps on her tummy*] Hello! Anybody home?

PAT   Stop it, Lionel.

LIONEL   Why? Sh! I want to hear my son's heart beating. [*Listens*]

PAT   [*Laughing*] Don't be so silly. You can't hear it like that.

LIONEL   [*Straightening up suddenly*] Hey! He kicked me! The little . . . right in my face. My own son!

PAT   [*Laughing*] It serves you right.

LIONEL   Pat. What you think our son will look like, eh? A douglah mother and an even more mixed-up father. . . . Did I ever tell you that my grandfather was a pork-knocker? Part African and part Amerindian? He disappeared somewhere up the Demerara River. . . .

PAT   Yes. Yes. [*As to a child*] And your grandmother was a Portuguese from Madeira and your maternal grandfather was an Indian from India. . . . You know, sometimes I believe you made up that whole family tree you always talking about. Besides [*Kissing him on the forehead*] your son may turn out to be a daughter. [*Gets up*] What do you want to eat?

LIONEL   Coffee, eggs, toast: Whatever we have. You were right! I'm hungry.

PAT   No eggs. How about some smoked herring? There's some left.

LIONEL   Perfect [*She goes out.*] And don't worry about this mess [*Calling up to her*] I'll clear it up.

[*He goes over s.r., picks up empty carton and starts putting bottles, etc. in it. Puts box on table then goes over to* Robe *painting. Facing u.s., takes off sunglasses and puts hand over eyes, sitting as if suddenly dizzy. He is facing the painting. Rises, puts on sunglasses and exits carrying carton.*]

DIM OUT

Part Two

The Game of the Stone

Scene Three

Lights come up on a forest clearing at night. As in opening scene except that now it is a pork-knocker's camp. There is a small lean-to in the background, its occupant asleep in a hammock (as in scene one). A pork-knocker sits by a smouldering fire which sends a thin wisp of smoke curling upwards. In front of him is a wooden crate on which rests a bottle af white rum, enamel cups, etc. He takes occasional swigs. He is already well-oiled, but not too unsteady. He gets up anxiously to look at the sleeping figure. He is awaiting someone's return. There is a sudden noise, like a cough, near at hand, and the man reaches for his torch, shines its beam towards the wings (s.r.) Nothing happens. He is just turning away when the noise is repeated. He turns suddenly.

MERGENCY   Santos? [*A hoarse whisper*]

SANTOS   [*2nd pork-knocker enters carrying a torch and shot-gun He has a small shovel strapped to his pack. He is tired and out of breath.*] Is me. You expecting somebody else? [*Indicates figure in hammock as he rids himself of gun, pack, etc.*] Buckman John-O still sleeping off all dat liquor wha e knack dung dis af'noon? [*Sits on crate and pours a shot. Swallows it*]

MERGENCY   [*Surprised at* SANTOS'S *apparent calm. Angry at his own nervousness*] Shit man Santos, ah des jus beginning foh tink is lass you get lass or something. [*No answers from* SANTOS] Well? w'appen? you fine de ting? [*He begins to sense that there is something odd about his partner's manner.*]

SANTOS   Nah. Ah din fin no stone. [*He speaks slowly and deliberately like someone unsure of his ability to explain a strange personal failing.*] You en too far wrong dough

pardna. Is nearly lass ah lass me SELF. Out deh coal and
dark like hell self, yeh. An dig dig round deh weh you
tell me seh you see e hide um till sweat start for get
cole, cole pun me back like Kinaima han'self. In de
darkness – so dark you feel like you gone blin' – ah
hear the river running and the sound of de bush like if
was a . . . a sorta music. Like if de river an de trees
and de rocks – dem like they singing: An me heart
beating like a drum all de time. Den, eh, eh! Sudden-
sudden so me head begin to swim. Everyt'ing start foh
dance in front me eye – all roun' me, ah tell you. . . .
All de bush an' de trees-dem. An' it cole, cole, COLE.
Me bady start foh TRIMBLE . . . me teet' all chatterin'
in me head, ah tellin' you. An' ah remember again a
whole heap o' things wha' happen when ah was a lil'
boy. How me mudder use to cry when me fadder
gettin' ready foh go back in the bush an' 'e just would
watch her quiet so an' say: 'The life of a man does
dance to de music of de forest'. An' sudden-so me bady
start feel warm again. Ah smell the river-water, sweet
an' heavy, an' ah feel like if somebady watchin' me. . . .
You know how ah mean? Ah look up through the
trees an' ah see de moon comin' out from behin' a
cloud like a big gold coin. . . . Ah get a good, good
feelin'. You know? Like if de whole WORL' belongst to
me. De river, de trees, de sky, de MOON even. Dey
belongst to me. More dan all de gol' an' diamon' wha
deh in dis river an' creek . . . [*He comes to himself*] One
big lizard rass drap pun me neck an' ah t'ought was
labaria. Shite, me heart nearly stap beatin', yeh! Ah
mek wan jump so . . . [*Acts it out*] an' brush um off,
but de torchlite fall dung an' de dam bulb bruck pun
a sharp stone. Good t'ing is moonlite night tonight.

MERGENCY An you din fin nutten at all?

SANTOS Nat one ting. Dark like hell self down deh, yeh. Ah
mek bout two, tree wrong turn tryin foh fin de camp
trail. As ah deh comin round by monkey jump deh ah
sure ah hear tiger cough in de bush. You sure you see
Buckman fine something? You sure you eye ent playin'
tricks?

MERGENCY [*Steadily but not without effort*] Ah see 'e wid dis same two eye wha ah seein you wid now. Ah tell you is a big, big carat-stone wha 'e fine when we did wukkin down by rack pint [*Rock Point*] Ah SEE 'e, when 'e din tink nobady wasn't watchin 'e, hide un in 'e clothes and den seh how he gine an tek a shit. Ah sure is bury um in dem same bushes or by dem big raks. You look deh too?

SANTOS Ow, man! Ah look everywhere seh wheh you tell me. Me en fine one ting [*Drinks*] Out deh cole, yeh. An um dark like hell. [*Pauses*] So you tink Buckman John-O trying fe shit we up?

MERGENCY Lissen me man. You 'member is how much certificate an papah we had was fo sign fo get dis claim? An how Buckman John-O din want we sign?

SANTOS Because 'e did want we work it different . . .

MERGENCY [*He is getting tight. His gestures are elaborate, heavy, slack*] Ow, lissen me marn. Shit! Ah tellin you Someting. Buckman din wan come in wid we. You carn memorise dat? 'E did wan' each man wuk um fo 'eself . . .

SANTOS All o we did want um so at de start . . .

MERGENCY [*Waving aside the interruption*] . . . but Government Commissioner Office seh No. You un'stan me good? Her Majesty assifer seh it gat to be co-operative venture an we gat fo write dung all de gol' wha we fine in gol' book fo dey inspector dem, befo papah can sign. Buckman din like dat an now 'e trying fo trick we.

SANTOS But is Buckman who first tell we 'bout dis place.

MERGENCY Fo USE we! You eye blin' or what? you ent see how 'e does get quiet-quiet like today self when we comin back a rak pint? Like 'e seeing spirit? Ah bet 'e tell we wheh de nugget stone hide if we threaten fo shoot 'e Carib tail.

SANTOS   [*Surprised at* MERGENCY'S *anger and suspicious of his real motive*] But wait, wait. Mergency, is why you don' like this man so? Wha Buckman do you mek you goin' on so? 'E pore and black like we, man. Why you and dis buck-nigger always like fowl-cock an' cackroach?

MERGENCY   Santos, you tekking up fo 'e! You tellin me ah lie! ME! Jonas Mergency!

SANTOS   [*He has taken out the 'makings' and lit his pipe.*] Cool dung, man. I en seh you lie. All t'ree o we gat dis claim an is all t'ree a we gat fo play dis game. If Buckman fine carat-stone an hide um an don' wan tell we we boun' fo ketch 'e sooner ar later when 'e en tink we gat we eye pun 'e. Don' worry you head 'bout dat, pardnah.

MERGENCY   Don' worry? Don' worry, nuh? You gine wait til dis trickster bitch gan wid we gol'? Like 'e gat you head kufuffle wid all dem nancy-story 'bout 'e African fadder an 'e Amerindian mudder: how dey live pun tap Ayanganna til de day when dey fall down de mountainside an dead. De liard! De damn t'ief!! [*Gets up unsteadily*]

SANTOS   Wheh you tink you goin? Look, sit dung . . .

MERGENCY   [*Picks up shot-gun*] De t'ief! 'E gat de stone hide somewheh [*Moves shakily towards hammock*] an if he don' tell we wheh 'e hide um ah gine shoot 'e backside. HI! YOU! BUCKMAN JOHN-O!!

SANTOS   [*Trying to take gun away*] Mergency, you mad black fool! . . . Gimme de dam gun . . .
[*The weird music of Scene I fades in growing gradually louder*] Wait, WAIT, YOU FOOL!! Listen! . . . [*As they stand absolutely still, staring towards the bush, a low rumbling growl is heard.*]

MERGENCY   What de hell . . .

SANTOS   OH JESUS IS A TIGER!!!! [*They run off.*]

Scene Four

The music stops and another sound takes over. The sound of cymbals clashed [but not fully], a length of metal sheeting being shaken, a low, electronic whine ascending rapidly to an ear-splitting pitch. At the climax, on the final full clash of cymbals, a tall African wearing Ashanti priest's robes, carrying a long stick, his head and face covered with a black cloth, enters stage right. The lighting colour changes to blue. At this point there is only the sound of the Ntumpane: the Ashanti talking drums. An African boy, AN ATTENDANT, *bears a ceremonial stool, vessels.*

PRIEST   [*Sits on stool which is placed centre stage for him. He raises the long staff and the drums stop. His movements are deliberate, slow and very gentle. He addresses the audience as if speaking to children.*] Mahengwana. [*He removes his 'mask' to reveal his face decorated with white lines to resemble the markings of a jaguar.*] Mukhubela wa hantana. Clouds come from all parts. Gajimare [*Points upward*] is angry with his wife, Uwardowa, forest-mother. [*Puts finger to lips*] Ntshengu. Ntshengu! [*The equivalent of 'hush'*] All will be well. In the morning when the sun comes up you will see Masharua – the spider's rainbow. Ntshengu! Ba hela hi shiruba, All will be well. [*Traces with staff on ground*]
The stream crosses the path
the path crosses the stream:
which of them is the elder?
Did we not cut a path to go and meet this stream?
The stream had its origin long ago.
The stream had its origin in the Creator.
He created things.
The great lord Tano. [*Tah-no*]
[*He rises.* ATTENDANT *hands him a gourd-shaped vessel.* PRIEST *holds it heavenward*]
Nyankonpon Tweaduapon 'Nyame, gye nsa nom
Supreme god of the sky upon whom men lean and do not fall,
receive this wine and drink.
Asase ya, gye nsa nom.

Earth mother, receive this wine and drink
[*Pours a libation*]
Nsasamanfo, munye nsa nom.
Spirit of our ancestors, receive this wine and drink.
[ATTENDANT *hands him a small pouch like a coin-case*]
Ta Yao, god of goldmakers, honoured among the sons
of Tano, we offer you this dust of gold in
remembrance of Anotchi's gift to Osai Tutu.
Damirifa!
Damirifa!
Let the golden stool, spirit of our ancestors, sunsum
of our ancestors,
Descend again.
Kokokyinaka bird who taught our drums to speak,
Where is it that you are?
Let the ntumpane speak! [*Sound of drums*]
Give answer to our greeting great Ta Kora for we
are addressing you, and you will understand.
Father of the people,
we sleep at the crossroads.
It is as the tiger that we walk.
The tiger is in the thicket, seeks a path.
We are addressing you, O Tano
You will understand.
We are addressing you
and you will understand.
Odomankoma 'Kyerema se
Osore anopa a, obe yan anopa.
We are addressing you and you will understand.
[*Lights dim gradually during last sentences to blackout.
Music fades in. Flute melody first added to existing
drum rhythm, then add cymbals gently shaken in time,
and, finally, chinese bells. Fade to end scene.*]

Scene Five

LIONEL'S *studio. Bright daylight outside. Dogs barking in background.
A loud-speaker van passes slowly with a repeated message which grows
louder then fades as the van recedes:*

'There will be a meeting of the People's National
Party tonight at eight o'clock at the corner of Church
Street and Stone Avenue. The public is invited to
attend. Everyone welcome. There will be a meeting. . . .
etc.'
*A car drives up, stops, slamming of doors, etc. Voices off.
Scene in* LIONEL'S *studio. Figure in hammock stirs.*

EDDIE [*Off*] Hi! Pat. Where's your husband? Still asleep?

ARTHUR [*Off*] Hi, Pat.

PAT [*Off*] Hi! Lionel's in his studio. Lionel! [*We see* LIONEL *in studio in hammock stir and get up.*] [*To* EDDIE *&* ARTHUR]

LIONEL Hi. Come in. Come in. [EDDIE *enters stage left, a stocky douglah, affable and given to making banal jokes; followed by* ARTHUR, *a slim, neat Afro-Guyanese with an alert manner and a ready laugh. They are the 'Pork-knockers' of the previous scene.*]
Eddie, was it you put my shoes up on the '*Tacouba*' sculpture last night? [EDDIE *guffaws*] You could have broken the damn thing, you know.

EDDIE Lionel boy, you got a suspicious mind, you know. It was probably one of your drunkie friends . . . like old Arthur here.

ARTHUR [*To* LIONEL] Look. You sue him for damages and I'll sue him for libel.

EDDIE [*In mock disgust*] Well yes! Friends, boy, friends!

LIONEL You don't know Eddie. Sue him? He's probably got an insurance policy to cover being sued.

EDDIE [*Laughing*] Naw, boy. That's one kind of policy we don't offer. Too risky. But talking about insurance, Lionel. It's time you started thinking about another little policy, you know . . .

ARTHUR [*Groaning*] Oh Lord. You've started him off now.

EDDIE [*Taking out a tiny notebook, he flips through it rapidly.*] Let's see. How about a Family Endowment Scheme? You're soon going to be a family man, you know.

LIONEL Right. That's why I can't afford to spend any more money on insurance.

ARTHUR [*Laughing. Lights up a cigarette, offers* EDDIE *one.* LIONEL *does not smoke.*] If you ask me, Lionel, you ought to insure your work against vandalism. [*Lights* EDDIE'S *cigarette*]

EDDIE What about you Arthur? You ought to take out some insurance, man. Think of all that income tax you're paying out. Neville took out a nice policy with me, you know [*Flips pages*] Businessman's Whole of Life . . .

ARTHUR Look. My brother is a married man with five kids. He *needs* insurance, friend.

LIONEL Eddie. You don't offer insurance against marriage? I bet you Arthur would take out a big policy.

EDDIE You right! Arthur scared like hell of marriage, boy. Worse than death!

ARTHUR [*Good-naturedly*] O.K. Laugh. But you notice that insurance companies will cover you in case of accident or death. But not in the case of marriage. You ever wondered why?

LIONEL [*Enjoying himself*] No. Why?

ARTHUR Because marriage is TOO damaging boy. It involves not one, but two deaths.

EDDIE Pat and Lionel don't look dead to me.

ARTHUR [*Shrugs. Smiles*] Pat and Lionel are exceptions to the rule.

LIONEL Don't worry with Arthur. I know what his trouble is. School teachers' syndrome.

EDDIE School teachers' what?

LIONEL	Occupational disease. [*This to* ARTHUR] Overwork and underpay leading to cynicism and a generally jaundiced view of life. Right, Arthur? I suggest a drink. Beer?
ARTHUR	Thanks.
LIONEL	Beer for you too, Eddie?
EDDIE	Wait, goat bite me or something? Yes, thanks. [*This with unnecessary politeness*]
LIONEL	Right! Oh. I want you to look at my latest masterpiece [*Goes over to easel, brings it forward s.c. and turns it around*] See what you think. [*Goes over to door u.s. calls upstairs*] Pat!
PAT	[*Off*] Yes?
LIONEL	Coming down?
PAT	[*Off*] Yes! Just now.
LIONEL	Can you bring some beers from the fridge when you're coming?
PAT	[*Off*] O.K.!
LIONEL	[*To* EDDIE *and* ARTHUR *who have been looking at the painting*] Well, what do you think of it? I finished it after you all left last night. This morning!
ARTHUR	[*Laughs*] What? with all that liquor inside you?
EDDIE	What wrong with you, boy? Lionel paints best when the spirit moves him.
ARTHUR	What are you calling this one? [*Studying it closely*]
LIONEL	'Robe of Ancestors'.
ARTHUR	[*Stands back*] 'Robe of Ancestors'. You know, Lionel, I prefer it to that surrealistic 'Couvade' thing . . . [*Waves aside* LIONEL'S *attempted objections*] yes, I know you're going to say that I'm biased and so on; but this is. . . . Well, it's more down-to-earth. You know what I mean? I like the bold colours. And this heavy, solid brushwork here . . .

EDDIE   Ah. Now that was because of the liquor, you see. He didn't realise he was mixing the paint so thick. And you know how he always got on those dark glasses....

ARTHUR   Eddie. Why don't you sit down and take the weight off your brain for a while? Seriously though, Lionel, this is much more powerful stuff. Not so vague and dreamy. The THEME of the thing is more relevant. The idea of ancestors. Good! Amerindian myths and so on might be O.K. as fantasy, boy, but we have to be concerned with the Folk. With ROOTS. But wait. [*Laughs*] I notice that you couldn't resist bringing in your beloved Amerindian motifs [*Indicates point*] What is it? Timehri?

LIONEL   No. Actually it's from the designs used in Arawak weaving and basketwork. If you notice, the whole thing is mostly a blend of African and Amerindian motifs. But there are other elements, too. Indian, Chinese....

ARTHUR   [*Laughs*] Still the same old message, eh? 'Out of the many, one'. You're not committing yourself, as usual.

LIONEL   Does one have to?

ARTHUR   Lionel, you know that is a truly bourgeois attitude.

LIONEL   What is? To refuse to take up a position on one side of an imaginary fence?

ARTHUR   The middle-classes never *see* the fence boy, because they're always sitting on it. You know you remind me of those people who live on that tiny, volcanic island. Tristan De Cunha. Halfway between Africa and South America, cut off from both and mixed up like hell, but still determined to keep to themselves like a nation of hermits.

LIONEL   They have their own culture, however. Their own unique way of life. They're happy.

ARTHUR   Yes. And they're sitting on top of a volcano. [*Looks at painting again*] 'Robe of Ancestors', eh? You know, Lionel, a robe is meant to be worn. No work of art exists in a vacuum.

LIONEL [*Laughs*] Sounds as if you see it as a sociological painting. A political statement or something.

ARTHUR Why not?

LIONEL But I'm not interested in the Politics of Art or the Art of Politics. . . .

EDDIE [*Seated in the armchair stage centre, smoking a cigarette*] Don't tell me you-all back on that same old argument again?

LIONEL What do you think of it, Eddie?

EDDIE Me? Boy I'm no art critic. Tell me, though, What are all those faces supposed to be? Your ancestors?

LIONEL No. Eddie.

EDDIE They all staring into space as if they seeing spirits. I wouldn't like to meet any of them on a dark night, boy. Ancestors or no ancestors.

ARTHUR Of course you know Eddie doesn't believe in racial ancestry. He thinks he was specially created. And God said: let there be light . . . and dark . . . and mulatto . . . and douglah. Right, Eddie?

EDDIE Very funny. But what's the use getting all worked up about ancestors when most of us don't even know who our grandfather was? Some of us don't even know who our father was.

ARTHUR Speak for yourself, friend.

LIONEL Anyway, the painting is SUPPOSED to suggest the variety of ancestors that we all have. The mixture of different cultures out of which we can develop a uniquely GUYANESE culture. You seem to think, Arthur, that we should consider only the African element.

ARTHUR I don't think anything of the sort. Look. In which races you find the greatest number of the people in this country?

EDDIE The races at D'urban Park, not too long ago.

ARTHUR   ... Africans and Indians, right? Both of them cut off from their indigenous cultures, both suspicious of each other, afraid of losing even more of their identity. I'll tell you something. If Africans and Indians in this country don't FIRST come to terms with mother Africa and mother India: to know something about their own roots: they will NEVER come to terms with being Guyanese. They will always feel rootless. Always trying to relieve the itching of an amputated limb.

EDDIE   Ow, listen to the man, nuh? 'always trying to relieve the itching of an amputated limb'. Arthur boy, you ought to be a poet. Or a politician. Is a pity you can't be both, but I understand THAT is dangerous. Tell me something though. All of us born right here in Guyana, right?

ARTHUR   [*Humouring him*] Right!

EDDIE   Not in Africa or India. What the hell any of us know about those places? How you going to START to 'come to terms', as you put it, with places you never even SEEN?

ARTHUR   Lionel, how you could have this man as a brother-in-law? I am not talking about geography, Eddie. I'm discussing ethnic origin. Sociogenetics.

EDDIE   Beg your pardon, teacher, [*With elaborate humility*] but I thought your subject WAS Geography.

LIONEL   [*Amused*] He's got a point, Arthur ...

EDDIE   Thank you, brother-in-law.

LIONEL   If you had been born in New York or London you might have felt very different about mother Africa.

ARTHUR   What's that got to do with it?

PAT   [PAT *has entered with a tray of beers, three glasses, etc.*] What you all arguing about now?

EDDIE   You just in time, girl. These two at it again. [*Takes tray and puts on table up-stage begins opening and pouring beer*].

PAT   O Lord! Not another political . . . discussion! [*Sits in armchair c.s.*] You-all didn't have enough arguments last night? Look, try and talk about something else for a change.

ARTHUR   We were discussing your husband's latest masterpiece. Pat. What do you think of it?

PAT   Me? I don't know anything about art, and even less about Amerindian myths.

ARTHUR   Oh? [*A trifle smugly*] What's the myth behind this one Lionel?

LIONEL   It's very much like the Couvade myth, I'm afraid. [*Laughs*] Pure fantasy. You wouldn't be interested, Arthur.

EDDIE   [*Handing round drinks*] Don't worry with him, man, I still like nancy stories. Let's hear it.

ARTHUR   Look, Eddie, you better be careful how you speak. Nancy stories? Lionel takes these things seriously, hear?

LIONEL   It's nothing original. Quite a well known, so-called, pagan ritual still seen in many parts of the world. It's a ceremony in which the spirits of the dead are supposed to return and talk to the living. Through the meeting of past and present, a regeneration of the tribal consciousness takes place.

EDDIE   [*After a pause*] Yes. Well, you lost me long time, chief. Explain, somebody. Pat, you know what your husband talking about?

PAT   [*Laughs*] You'll have to ask him yourself.

ARTHUR   Sounds like Haitian vodun, Lionel.

EDDIE   You mean Voodoo!! I thought that was to do with sticking pins in little dolls. This conversation is definitely weird. [*Lights a cigarette, offers them round*]

ARTHUR   [*Taking a cigarette* EDDIE *lights it for him.*] But that's an African-inspired ritual, isn't it? Not an Amerindian thing.

LIONEL   African-inspired, yes. The point is, it's a CARIBBEAN thing.

ARTHUR   Well, this idea about the past having some mystical effect on our lives is all very nice and poetic. We know a good deal about our past, though, and it isn't very pretty. Or poetic. We don't need to have our ancestors come back and talk to us to know that slavery was hell. We KNOW it was. For that matter, Caribs and African slaves weren't exactly bosom friends, you know. For all I know my great-grandfather might well have been hunted down in the forest by one of these Amerindian ancestors you're always talking about.

PAT   But perhaps he escaped. Perhaps he even held down some poor Amerindian girl in the bush.

EDDIE   Or perhaps SHE held HIM down. You never know.

LIONEL   As a matter of fact, Arthur, there WERE cases of Caribs and Africans living together and sharing a common culture . . .

ARTHUR   Jesus, you're not going to tell us again about your African great-grandfather and your Carib great-grandmother? Accidents happen, you know.

LIONEL   Have you ever heard of the Black Caribs of St. Vincent? No. Wait [*Goes towards bookshelf. Looks for book*] Let me read you something.

PAT   You-all will have to excuse me. I have my housework to think about. [*Gets up*].

EDDIE   Pat, you have any more beer in the fridge?

PAT   Yes, come up and get them, Eddie.

EDDIE   O.K. [*Picks up tray and follows her*]

LIONEL   Ah. Here it is. [*Reads*] 'The Black Caribs are, in the main, descendants of African Negroes brought to the West Indies as slaves, but who escaped from their European masters and took refuge among the island Carib in St. Vincent, subsequently adopting the latter's language, and to a considerable extent, culture. They emerged there as a distinct society at the beginning of the eighteenth century'.

ARTHUR Black Caribs? And they lived with the Indians and spoke their language?

LIONEL That's right. The Indians, were of Arawak/Maipuree stock and they accepted the runaway slaves as brothers. This man, Taylor [*Looks at spine of book*] is an American who made a study of the Black Caribs. Listen! [*Thumbs rapidly through book*] 'It is evident that those Negroes who, by chance or from design, sought refuge on the island of St. Vincent and later became the Black Carib, were treated as fellow citizens by their Indian hosts; and there is no reason to doubt that the brunt of the ensuing wars with the whites was borne equally by both races'.

ARTHUR Let's have a look at that. [*Takes book*]

LIONEL It's not just the odd case of Amerindian and African mixture – what they used to call a Buffianda. This is a whole new society: a unique culture . . .

ARTHUR Well, they certainly LOOK African. Not Amerindian.

LIONEL Yes, but their CULTURE, their whole way of LIFE, is a mixture of both. And they speak their own form of Carib dialect . . .

ARTHUR [*Puts down book*] Yes, but what's the point? So this man – this scientist or anthropologist or whatever he is – has discovered that Africans and Carib Indians lived side by side on this island and the Africans eventually became known as the Black Caribs.
[EDDIE *has entered at this point.*]

EDDIE What you-all talking about now? What's this about Black Arabs?

LIONEL Not Arabs, CARIBS.

EDDIE Black Caribs? [*Busy with drinks.*]

ARTHUR Black men who became Amerindians, believe it or not.

EDDIE   That's nothing, man. I know of black men who went abroad and became Europeans! You never heard about black Englishmen?

ARTHUR   You're right! The black man especially in the West Indies is forever trying to be someone else. He still doesn't TRUST his blackness. You see he just can't believe that its ALL RIGHT to be a black man. Read Frantz Fanon, man. 'Black skin, white masks'.

LIONEL   You're deliberately missing the point, Arthur.

ARTHUR   [*Beginning to show signs of belligerence*] What point? That a few runaway slaves, rather than live like animals under their white masters, chose to join forces with the Carib Indians? What's so surprising about that? They didn't change the colour of their skin!

LIONEL   Yes, but don't you see? Their whole CULTURE changed. Absorbed the Carib culture and became something NEW. THEIR descendants are no longer African OR Amerindian. Their children inherited the seeds of different cultures just as WE have from OUR ancestors. . . .

ARTHUR   Look. You're forgetting something. We all know that the white coloniser didn't simply rule by force. His prime object was to destroy the CULTURE of the colonised people – their roots! Even the Amerindians' culture was destroyed. It had already decayed a good bit anyway. It's no good just trying to pick up the pieces, the crumbs, that remain. We have to establish roots again. With Africa. With India . . .

EDDIE   [*Ticking them off on his fingers*] And China and Portugal and England and Holland . . . and wait, boy, one of my ancestors came from Syria, I believe.

LIONEL   Exactly. How do you decide which ancestors count and which don't?

ARTHUR   [*Angry now*] How? How? [*Points to his own arm, a theatrical gesture*] THIS is how. Whether you like it or not, you're black. You blind or something? Take off your shades, man, and look yourself good! You go to any one of the big, progressive white countries. 'Nigger go home'. That's the message, friend. Black people in the West Indies will ALWAYS be ashamed of their skin until they learn to accept Africa as a spiritual home. Only then will they have any real sense of power; power to stop the colonial brain-washing that STILL goes on, even in the minds of children. You and your tolerance! All this talk about the 'seeds of different cultures'. That is just a load of bullshit! Like your Amerindian myths.

EDDIE   Right. Let's change the subject, eh?

LIONEL Of course, YOU would be happier if they were African myths. Look, ALL myths about ancestors and so on are very much alike: and they're more important than you think. The point is, the Amerindian myths are NATIVE to Guyana. Like US. WE'RE native to Guyana! But of course you're too obsessed with colour to see that.

EDDIE   [*Trying to head off a clash*] O.K. O.K. Let's talk about something....

ARTHUR *I'm* too obsessed...?

EDDIE   Ow, cool down nuh, man?

ARTHUR What about you and your fairy tales? Wake up, man! That's for babies and CHILDREN, not for big men. [*Picks up the book and raps it with his knuckles – a deliberately provoking action*] As for THIS [LIONEL *moves to take it away.* ARTHUR *backs towards stage left where* PAT *has entered quietly and is standing unseen by* ARTHUR] This is written by a whiteman with the usual racist assumptions... [*As* LIONEL *lunges for the book,* ARTHUR *swings it away, hard, in a wide arc, hitting* PAT *a sharp blow in the stomach. She cries out and doubles up in pain.*]

LIONEL Pat! Pat!

EDDIE   [*To* ARTHUR] You bloody fool! [*They help her to armchair while* ARTHUR *stands stricken*]

ARTHUR O God, I didn't see her....

LIONEL	Eddie, get a doctor quickly. QUICK, man!
EDDIE	We could take her in the car . . .
PAT	(obviously in some pain) No. No, I'm all right.
ARTHUR	Christ, Lionel. I'm sorry. I just didn't see her . . . is she all right?
LIONEL	[*Not looking at him*] It was an accident. Pat, is it bad?
PAT	[*With great effort*] No. Help me upstairs.
LIONEL	Maybe you'd better stay here, love. We'll get a doctor to come. . . .
PAT	[*Angry now*] NO! Help me upstairs. [*Lionel helps her up, and they leave.* EDDIE *and* ARTHUR *remain, looking uncertainly at each other.*]

BLACKOUT

Scene Six

A single overhead lamp lights up a spot c.s. at the extreme edge of the stage apron. The effect is of a street corner lit by a solitary street lamp. Workmen directed by party official [played by stage crew and stage manager] come on to set up stage for a political meeting. Microphone and loudspeaker arranged [with inevitable electronic whinings and shouted directions of manager] and tested; lectern with party emblem installed, etc. The audience treated as the public at the meeting, waiting for the speaker to appear. The workmen leave. After a while, the speaker comes forward to the lectern with a sheaf of notes which he ostentatiously places on the lectern. He is the SHAMAN, *but 'disguised' by his baggy trousers, loose-fitting jacket and hat. His face is in shadow.*

MAN	Goodnight, comrades and friends. On behalf of the National Party I would like to say how pleased I am to see so many of you here tonight. As we all know, next week is General Elections week and it will once again be our duty – our inalienable right – to make our cross on that ballot paper. It will also be our duty – the duty of each and every one of us – to

examine, to search our hearts and our conscience before we go to the polls. For we also have a duty to see to it that we do not take lightly the privilege which is ours: the privilege to decide how and by whom we wish to be governed.

Comrades, it is not for me or for my party to tell you how you must vote. NO man, NO party, can arrogate that power unto itself. It is for YOU, having listened carefully to the arguments of ALL the parties, having satisfied yourselves as to the truth (or otherwise) of their statements and the validity of their promises and policies; it is for YOU to make up your own minds. This is YOUR right. This power is in YOUR hands alone. It is the power of the People, and it is up to you to exercise it.

HECKLER: ('speak louder, man, we can't hear you!') Now, I haven't come here tonight, comrades, to make big promises or to outline grand and sweeping policies which, however desirable, would, in practice, be totally unworkable and as such, an offence against commonsense. That would be a waste of your time and mine and an insult to your intelligence. I shall just ask you one simple question. Has any other party so consistently stood for Land Tenure reform? Or for government-aided self-help in the field of Agriculture? The answer, my friends, is NO. Yet without an enlightened agrarian policy, any talk about 'repossession of the interior' can be little more than an exercise in wishful thinking. The People's National Party has over and over again stressed this. That any continuous development of interior resources must finally depend on these two factors: the right to own the land and the incentive to put down roots. To live and to work on the land. For if the land is to be repossessed, it is the people who must repossess it.

Many of us here tonight, most of us, in fact, have small holdings here in Manoa; tiny footholds by means of which (who knows?) the great door of the interior will one day be opened. When that day comes, and, make no mistake, it WILL come! it will be due largely to YOUR efforts, YOUR sweat, YOUR toil. Of course there are still some misguided souls who cling to the old myth of El Dorado. The myth that says you can get rich without hard work. But you and I know different. We know that without honest, hard toil there can never be an El Dorado. That if we want to have an El Dorado we must create it ourselves, out of our own sweat, our own tears, our own dreams . . .

[*At this point, an electronic whine – a musical note – is barely audible, growing gradually louder as the pitch rises.*] Here in Manoa you have flung a stone into the water and the ripples have begun to move outwards, in wider and wider circles, touching everything in their path. [*His manner is becoming incantatory now. He is slowly metamorphosing into the* SHAMAN. *His voice also begins to change. The light begins to dim.*] Disturbing the surface of the water. Soon these ripples will touch the cities on the coast and people in their comfortable houses will feel the shock and be disturbed.

They will be afraid and begin to ask why. Why the surface of the water has been disturbed. Why their peace of mind has been shaken. But when the gold, lies at the bottom of the creek, how else is it to be reached? [*Sound ceases here.*] Yes comrades, the game of the stone is a dangerous game. For he who casts the stone must harbour no stone in his own heart. Blood travels a circular path. It always brings its poison home. [*As he speaks he traces a circle with one finger, in the air.*] Our country's heart is HERE, at Manoa. Here, where life is rooted in the earth and gold flows from the cultivation of the land, as milk flows from the udders of the cows . . .

[*Sound of scene one music fades in here*] Milk of the calabash. Manioc gruel. Milk of the land. And the land owes you a debt, comrades. How shall it be repaid?

Remember: The spider spins his web by day
           to catch industrious flies.
           The trickster promises to pay
           And swears the truth with lies.

[*Music out as jacket falls open. He is naked underneath.*

[Sounds of forest fade in. SHAMAN *steps upward and squats on top of lectern. He now assumes a deliberately ambiguous role, that of protagonist-narrator. The lighting here is directed upwards into* SHAMAN'S *face.]*
Let me tell you how the spider paid his debts: One night, before the moon start to sail across the sky, you know? . . . when the stars go visiting one another, Spider sent Lizard to tell all the animals that next day he, Spider, would pay them all back. Early next morning, Toucan came to collect his debt. Spider said 'Good, I will pay you, but wait inside the hut a minute while I pick some nice fruit for you.' While Toucan was waiting, Wildcat came to collect his debt. 'Good,' said Spider, 'go inside the hut and you will find payment.' Wildcat went and found Toucan and ate him up. Just then, Puma came to collect his debt. 'Good,' said Spider, 're-payment is inside the hut. Just go in and collect it.' So Puma went in and found Wildcat and ate him up. Just then, who should come to collect his debt but Tiger. 'Good,' said Spider, 'look in the hut and you will find repayment.' So the Tiger went in and found Puma and the two of them began to fight. Now when they were busy fighting, Spider took some pepper, climbed in through the window, and threw it in their eyes. Then he took a big stone and beat them until they were dead. Both of them. And that is how Spider paid his debts. [*Rises, goes down behind lectern and rises as the* POLITICIAN. *Forest sounds fade out.*]

My friends, I thank you for giving me so much of your time. I hope that when you return to your homes tonight you will think about these things I have said to you [*His manner now is as it was when the speech began.*] And when the time comes for you to place your cross, like a black spider [*makes the* SHAMAN'S *ritual gesture with his open palm and fingers*] on that ballot-paper, I hope you will remember what you have heard here tonight. I thank you.

BLACKOUT

Part Three

The Masque of Ancestors

Scene Seven

A totally darkened stage. A shaft of light illuminates the bed on which LIONEL *and* PAT *are seen asleep as on a raft afloat on the darkness.* LIONEL *tossing from side to side. He is having a nightmare. Music is heard faintly, in the distance, approaching gradually. A rhythmic sound of cymbals and Chinese chime-bells shaken lightly.* LIONEL *rises, eyes closed as in a dream, and sits on the edge of the bed, stiffly, trance-like. Spot gradually comes up on the hooded Ashanti priest who stands on a small platform painted black so as to be invisible: the effect of standing in mid-air. He uses gesture sparingly, and speaks in a slow, rhythmic, incantatory voice. The light in which he stands should [if possible] cast undulating or revolving patterns on his robe as he speaks. The music remains as a background accompanient to the dream.*

LIONEL   [LIONEL *in shorts only – naked from waist up*] Who are you? [*Without opening his eyes. His voice has the tonelessness associated with hypnosis.*]

PRIEST   I am many things. And nothing. A shadow.
The shadow that rises with you when you wake
and runs before you in the morning:
the wedge of darkness that you stand on
when the sun is overhead;
that walks behind you when night comes.
I am your dark reflection sleeping at the bottom
of a pool,
rising to meet you when you look;
words in a book, cold water of a creek;
the dreams of sleepers in their hammocks by the fire;
gold and diamonds, waterfalls, the rivers that all
dreamers seek, all men desire.
And I have been the silent song of the Guacharo bird,

the eyes that watch the traveller from the darkness
of the trees:
The wind that comes like rain among the leaves:
the beating of your heart.
I have been all of these.
There is nothing that I have not been.
I am part of your dream.
Only a dream.

[*Light dims and goes out as spot comes up slowly on* SHAMAN, *masked, on another platform.*]

SHAMAN I, too, am part of your dream. I have been many
things before.
The drops of water hanging from a spider's web
like jewels after rain:
a lizard scampering across the forest floor,
the cry of the Tukuiu bird:
I have been all these things and more.
I have flown with the hawk towards the sun,
run with the deer
blown with the seeds of the silk-cotton tree,
spinning, turning in air.
I have been the fish that leaps
suddenly
in the dark
revealing the light in the stream:
I am part of your dream.
Only a dream.
Look! [*Points dramatically as dancers, bodies draped in black, masked, only bare feet and hands visible, appear moving with ritualistic gestures beneath the hooded figure of the* DREAMER, *who is dressed to look exactly like* LIONEL. *He is seated cross-legged in the hammock, arms outstretched u.s. centre, lit from directly above.*]
See! Couvade sleeps. Son of Makanater sleeps. WE
are his dreams. All the old ones, all the young ones,
all the women, all the men, all the little ones, all the
great ones. Everything.that lives; plants, trees. Dust
of manioc, milk of the land, fruit of the earth. He
dreams us all. When he awakes, we die. The dream is
over. [*Spot dims, goes out*]

LIONEL *rises, moves like a blind man towards the figure of the dreamer. The dancers move their hands with out-stretched fingers, like a wall of trees – a warning gesture – and as* LIONEL *falls on his knees, reaching out towards his dreaming self, the light begins to fade. The music stops as the light goes out. When the light on the bed comes up again we see* LIONEL *tossing as before. He wakes with a cry and switches on the bedside lamp.*

PAT [*Surfacing from sleep, wincing at the sudden light*] LIONEL? What's wrong?

LIONEL I was having a nightmare. Sorry I woke you up, love. You go back to sleep.

PAT What was it, Lionel? The same dream again?

LIONEL Yes. [*Bitterly*] The same dream. It always seems so REAL!

PAT I'm sorry, darling. [*Puts her hand on his shoulder, turns to him and lies back against the headboard, her head on his chest*]

LIONEL Why should I dream this same dream night after night? It's weird, Pat.

PAT You ought to go and see the doctor about this trouble you have sleeping. And all these nightmares.

LIONEL But what would I tell him? 'Doctor, I have this recurring nightmare. Every night I dream that I awake and see myself dreaming and I can't wake myself up . . .' You can imagine what he would think!

PAT [*Sleepily*] But he could give you some sleeping pills or something . . . ?

LIONEL That might only make matters worse. You go back to sleep, love [*Kissing her on the forehead*] I'll be all right.

PAT O.K. But you try and get some sleep too. Don't go downstairs and do any work. Or stay up and hurt your eyes reading.

LIONEL All right, Pat. Go back to sleep. I'm sorry I woke you up.

PAT   [*Half asleep already*] Mmmm . . .'s all right.

            [LIONEL *switches lamp off, lies back. After a while there is, once again, the distant sound of cymbals and bells. The sound grows gradually nearer.*]

LIONEL   [*In a tight whisper*] Pat! [*No answer*] Pat! [*The sound stops.*]

PAT   Mmmm? What's the matter now?

LIONEL   [*Switches on lamp. She winces.*] Didn't you hear it?

PAT   Hear what?

LIONEL   That sound. Like little bells. It's gone now, but I heard it. The same sound I heard in my dream. And I wasn't dreaming it. I was wide awake.

PAT   It must have been something passing outside in the street.

LIONEL   [*A note of panic has crept into his voice.*] No! It was in this room. I HEARD it. Pat. Something's happening to me. My mind. Something's wrong.

PAT   [*Sitting up, she takes his head in her hands, turns him to her*] Now Lionel, don't you start worrying yourself for nothing. [*She cradles his head on her breast.*] Nothing is wrong with you except that you work far too hard and you don't get enough sleep. Promise that tomorrow you're going to see the doctor about it. Please? And let him give you something to make you SLEEP.

LIONEL   God! I'm beginning to feel almost AFRAID of falling asleep. . . .

PAT   Lionel, promise me you'll go and see the doctor tomorrow.

LIONEL   Yes. Yes. Maybe you're right. I can't go on like THIS.

PAT   Of course I'm right. Now try and get some SLEEP! [*She reaches across him and switches off the lamp.*]

Scene Eight

Early afternoon. The tiny living/dining-room of PAT'S *father. The 'old man' [in his late fifties] sits in the central rocking-chair, walking-stick within reach, newspaper open on his lap. He is scraping and knocking out his pipe. Everything – the drop-leaf table, old-fashioned sideboard, threadbare rug: even the potted plants in their small, brass containers – has that comfortable, much-used, dark-polished look which comes from a mixture of poverty and good husbandry. The doilies on table and sideboard are heavily hand-made, brightly coloured, vulgar. Prominently displayed on sideboard are a large, ornate, brass tray, like a burnished sun, and several brass figurines – [Indian elephants, little gods, etc.] General atmosphere suggests early twentieth century lower/middle class home. Small chime-bells hang just above open window. The tinkling sound of these, shaken by the wind, is heard on and off in the background right through the scene. A knock at the door.*

FATHER [*Turning stiffly*] Yes? Who's that?

PAT [*Her head appears at the open window as she leans across from outer stairs.*] It's me, daddy. Pat.

FATHER [*Turns his body round without rising. Reaches for stick and attempts to rise*] Eh, eh! It's you, Patricia?

PAT [*She has already opened door, come up and kissed him on forehead.*] Yes. Your long-lost daughter.

FATHER [*Taking her hand in both of his*] Well, look at this thing! I thought my eyes were playing tricks on me. How you do, child? How you do? Come, come. Sit down and tell me how you getting on. It's a long time I haven't seen you. You're scarce like gold dust.

PAT [*Sits, puts her bag in her lap. A trifle shy now she is facing him*] You're looking well, daddy.

FATHER And you're looking more than well. [*Chuckles*] Making this baby like it's really agreeing with you. Everything going all right?

PAT Yes, thanks. I'm fine. Oh, [*Looks in bag*] before I forget. Look. I brought you some of your favourite tobacco. [*Gives him a brown paper parcel*] I don't

35

	know how you can smoke that thing. It smells like vanilla and liquorish.
FATHER	[*Laughs: an indulgent 'hey hey' and takes parcel*] Rupununi black tobacco? They have nothing that smokes sweet like this thing, child. [*She makes a face.*] Better than all the new-fashion tobacco with fancy names. [*He sniffs the parcel, puts it on the table*] Many thanks, hear?
PAT	How is the leg behaving? You still manage to take your walks?
FATHER	The leg isn't too nice these days, but I'm still trying with the early morning walks. Sometimes Eddie takes me out for a little drive, you know. You only just missed him. He's not too long ago gone out.
PAT	[*Obviously disappointed*] Oh. You know when he's coming back?
FATHER	Child, I can't tell you. The car is giving him a little trouble and he's taken it to this friend who knows how to repair these things. The two of them always loosing the car down and playing mechanics. No wonder the thing giving trouble. So, Patricia girl. You come to look up the old man. I don't see you much these days. And how is Lionel? He's still with the art and the painting? Eddie says when he last saw your husband he looked like a walking ghost.
PAT	Yes. He's getting thin. Nowadays he's working day and night.
FATHER	Day and night? What he's doing so?
PAT	He wants to put on an exhibition and a lot of paintings still have to be finished. When he comes home from the school it's straight into his studio he goes. If you see the confusion in there! The whole house is beginning to smell like a paint-shop.
FATHER	Exhibition, eh? Hmn. I hope he's not neglecting you, child, what with the baby coming and so on. All this art and so is all very well, but first things always first.

	He's soon going to be a family man with responsibility. You getting enough rest and proper food and so on?
PAT	[*Subdued*] Yes, daddy. I'm all right.
FATHER	You have to think of the baby now, you know. The first one always the hardest. I don't know why you young people wait so long to start a family. People should have children young, so they can grow up with they children. Your mother, God rest her soul, was nineteen when Eddie was born. We had to do without a lot of things, but we still manage; and you and your brother didn't want for anything . . .
PAT	Things are different now, you know. Times change.
FATHER	They CHANGE all right! You only have to look around you to see how the times changing. How everybody trying to get rich till they stealing and killing each other for they money. Like nobody wants to do an honest day's work anymore. And the young people of today getting married and divorcing so quick just as how they clothes change with the fashion. And what happens? The children grow up and turn criminals. Times changing all right. [*Sighs*] When your mother was alive and you and your brother were little we used to have some happy times, even though the two of you used to lead us a dance [*Laughs*]. Eddie always up to some mischief . . .
PAT	[*Smiling*] Well HE hasn't changed much.
FATHER	. . . and you always taking up for him. You were a funny child. When Eddie was getting licks YOU used to cry as if it was you who was getting the blows. And you remember how you used to dress up in your mother's clothes? [*Laughs*] Only four years old and already you wanted to be a big woman.
PAT	Ow daddy, all children like dressing up.
FATHER	But YOU used to take it so serious! I remember once when you were finished dressing up how you climbed up to see yourself in the wardrobe mirror and the chair slip and you fell and get that mark on your

forehead. We didn't know which was the reason you cry more – whether it was the fall or that you didn't get to admire your reflection in the mirror. That day you cry the whole day nearly, till you cry out all the tears inside you . . . how the years they fly, eh? Now you're a big woman soon having children of your own. You know, seeing you here so grown up and with a whole new life growing inside you, I think I'm seeing your mother again . . . You take after her a lot, child. [*While he speaks* PAT *is toying with the gold bangle on her wrist.*] That used to be your mother's. That gold bangle.

PAT Yes. I know.

FATHER She wore it the day we married. You know, [*Chuckles*] it's twice we married that day. Not one, but TWO weddings. Indian wedding and church wedding. *I* tell you! We were well and truly married. Even now, though it's so long ago, I still remember the sweety-sweety smell of the incense-sticks – I believe that's why I so like this tobacco. It reminds me of that scent. [*Holds pipe out, looking at it*] And your mother in her wedding sari looking just like a princess . . . [*He is becoming sentimental. Checks himself*] But come, I'm talking too much. Let me get you a little something to eat. What about a piece of cake? Or some sweet biscuits?

PAT [*Rising to stop his attempt to get up*] No. You sit down and let me do that. I know where to find the things. Would you like some tea to go with it?

FATHER [*Subsiding gratefully*] Thank you, child. But don't trouble yourself to make tea . . .

PAT It's no trouble. You just sit yourself right there. I won't take two minutes [*Goes off*].

FATHER [*Laughs*] It's just so your mother used to like to boss me. [*Raising volume*] Some boiling water is there in the big flask. [*He takes up paper*] Patricia! you saw in today's paper about the P.N.P. man who they beat up after the meeting last night? They say it was two

	young hooligans. One of them pick up a stone and nearly crack open the man skull. Hell of a thing. I just don't know what this country is coming to.
PAT	[*Appears at doorway*] That's why I HATE politics. As soon as people start playing with politics somebody gets hurt. I don't see any sugar. You know if there's any?
FATHER	Oh, yes. In the 'fridge. In one of those little plastic boxes. [*She goes off*] I have to hide everything from these little fine ants. They're getting everywhere. They're even following the soap. Now when I go to bathe my skin I have to wash the soap off first, it so full of ants. Everything like it topsy-turvy nowadays. I don't know it's since when ants like soap. [*Pat enters with tray, he puts away paper and clears space on table*] Let me move this so you can put it down here. [*Notices single cup*] You're not having any tea?
PAT	[*Suddenly depressed*] No, thanks.
FATHER	Well, what about a sweet drink then? There's some in the . . .
PAT	No thanks, daddy. I'm all right. [*Stabs at her cake*] This is fine.
FATHER	You shouldn't have gone to the trouble to make just the one cup for me. You want to spoil me, eh? [*Sips tea noisily. Takes a bit of cake, daintily, with fingers. Picks up paper again.* PAT *goes over to sideboard. Picks up one of the small ornaments, looks at herself in the sideboard mirror.* FATHER *rests paper in lap, turning slightly to her*] What's the matter, Patricia? Like something worrying you.
PAT	[*Turning her head*] No. It's nothing.
FATHER	Anything wrong between you and Lionel?
PAT	[*Taken by surprise. She comes over and stands just behind him.*] What? No. Well . . . not exactly. [*She puts one hand on his shoulder*] Look. Daddy, would you mind if Eddie came and spent a couple of days with us?

FATHER [*Without looking up he reaches up to hold her hand.*] What's wrong, child? He's treating you badly?

PAT Who, Lionel? Oh no. It's nothing like that. It's just that . . . well, he's so wrapped up in his work and recently he's acting so strange . . .

FATHER [*With a touch of paternal severity*] You wish ME to have a few words with him? If all that art and painting gone to his head . . .

PAT [*She comes round in front of him.*] Daddy, I'm worried about him. His health. He won't listen to me and go to see a doctor. The painting seems to have him like if he's in a different world . . .

FATHER It sounds to me as if what he wants is a good shaking to wake him up!

PAT He's not well. And daddy, it's his eyes too . . .

FATHER His eyes?

PAT [*Her eyes have begun to fill with tears.*] Yes. [*She sits*] He won't listen to me and I thought if Eddie . . . Daddy, if he goes on like this much longer I'm afraid he's going to go blind. [*She is crying openly now.*]

FATHER [*Taking her hand as she wipes the tears with the other. He has leant forward and they are close together.*] Now now now. Don't you go worrying and upsetting yourself. Come come, tell me all about it. Look, [*Takes a handkerchief from trouser pocket*] dry your eyes. [*She does and blows her nose loudly as well.*] What's all this about Lionel's eyes?

PAT Oh daddy, his eyes are bad, bad. And he gets these terrible nightmares . . . he hardly gets any sleep when the night comes. If you see him! He's as thin as a ghost.

FATHER [*Furiously, on his daughter's account*] But what's wrong with him at all? He's trying to kill himself or what?

PAT And it's not only his eyes. He says he gets a kind of . . .

ringing noise inside his head sometimes, and he hears these . . . these voices . . .

FATHER But what's this you're saying, child? He's HEARING things? . . . voices?

PAT In his dreams. And he cries out and wakes up soaking with sweat.

FATHER And you say he doesn't want to go and see a doctor?

PAT [*Letting it all come tumbling out*] He went once about two weeks ago and the doctor gave him some tablets but they didn't seem to help. And now he says he's not going back. I went to see this doctor – Lionel doesn't know – and he said he thinks Lionel should see some nerve specialist or other. A friend of his. He said he could arrange the appointment. But I can't even get Lionel to go back and see HIM. He spends so much time in his studio painting, that sometimes he doesn't even want to eat. I thought if Eddie could come and stay a couple days or so he might be able to get Lionel's mind off the work for a bit. When Lionel comes home in the afternoon he won't even sit down and talk to me . . . Daddy, if you see his eyes! [*Tears have come again*] They're red like fire behind his shades.

FATHER [*Gets up with difficulty, using stick, and stands protectively over her, hand on her shoulder*] Come, Patricia. Don't take on so. Don't go worrying yourself too much over it. It wouldn't do you any good and it wouldn't do the baby any good. Everything going to be all right. When Eddie comes in I will tell him what you say. I think it's a good idea if he could stop at you and Lionel for a couple days. [*She looks up at him.*] Don't you worry about me. I will manage all right. [*Starts to go towards sideboard*]

PAT [*Turning to follow his progress, fishing hanky from bag*] Daddy, you're sure?

FATHER [*Places stick against sideboard and bends to take, from cupboard, an ancient bottle and two tiny glasses*] Of

41

course I'm sure! Tomorrow morning you will be surprise to see how everything going to look much brighter. Let me give you a taste of this special jamoon wine. [*Pours as he talks*] It will cheer you up a bit. You know, your dear mother always liked my jamoon wine, [*Brings glass for her. She gets up to meet him halfway*] she used to say how I trying to turn her into a drunkard [*Chuckles*] and I always used to tell her, 'Beena, this thing strengthens the heart and purifies the blood, hear?' And she would laugh ... [*He has fetched his glass and they stand c.s. near the table.*] I was keeping this bottle. Saving it up to wet the baby head. But we could take a little drop now, eh?

PAT I'm sorry I behaved like such a baby just now ...

FATHER Nonsense, child. You forget you're still a baby to me? Come. Let's have a toast. [*Raises glass*] Good health and happiness to you, daughter, and to your husband, Lionel, and to my future grandchild. What you say?

PAT Health and happiness to you too, daddy.

FATHER [*With deep sincerity, gently: almost like a benediction*] To all of us child. To all of us. [*They drink.*]

BLACKOUT

Scene Nine

Night. A street corner. Traffic noises, dogs barking, etc. The source of light is a single overhead street lamp. A small group of Jordanite sisters led by an imposing, bearded brother accompanied by a small boy [*they are the Ashanti Priest and his attendant*] *come on and set up table with candles and a gigantic Bible, oily black with use. The women and boy all wear the traditional white flowing robes with a head band from which a white cloth falls backwards, covering the head. The leader is regally attired in spotless white robe, still newly creased, his trousers and shoes just visible. He wears heavy bead necklaces and an elaborate, turban-like head-dress. He carries a ceremonial staff, like a shepherd's crook which gleams smooth as mahogany. He gives the impression of both clownishness and immense dignity. The group forms almost a half circle on either side of the table at which the preacher stands with the boy at his side. One of the older sisters begins a hymn in an uncertain, metallic, high-pitched soprano voice ['Whosoever will . . .'] and is followed by another who slaps a tambourine in time to the music. Gradually, all the women are singing. The preacher stands immobile, rock-like. Passers-by occasionally stop. [A man towing a small child on his bicycle: an old woman with a basket on her head: two mischievous small boys] But they eventually move on. When the hymn comes to an end, another sister comes up to the side of the table, picks up the huge Bible and reads a passage from it in a loud, cracked voice.*

SISTER   Hear the words of de praphet Ezekiel: Dus set de Lord. 'Dou hast DESPISE mine holy tings and hast PROFANED my sabbats. De people of de lan' have use oppression an' rabbery, an' have VEX de poor an' needy. Yea derefore have I CONSUME dem with de FIRE of my wrath. . . !'
[Desultory murmur of 'halleluia' from one or two sisters. Speaker puts Bible down and begins an original and spirited exegesis of the text. Much use of gesture and timing. She is a performer aware of her audience, supported by an able 'chorus'.]

SISTER   You hear what de good Book say? It say the Lord will CONSUME the unrighteous in de FIRES of everlastin' hell. Those who don't want to turn from they ungodly ways: de drinkin' an' swearin' an' uncleanness which is an abomination to de Lord – He will SMITE dem down! An don't tink dat you can HIDE your sins from Him. Vengeance is MINE, set de Lord. Dere is no REST for de wicked. All de rabbery an' violence dat goes go on today: de SINFULNESS what de young people goes in for: settin' they face against they parents – is DAT will turn dis country into another BABYLON! If a nation drink of de wine of the wrath of FORNICATION an' LUXURY it will become de habitation of DEVILS. When people turn away from de Lord is STRAIGHT into de arms of de Devil dey goin'. To everlastin' PERDITION an' de bottomless pit. You have to choose. You cannot serve two masters. De Lord Jehova made de Heavens and lay de foundations of de earth. He say to the children

43

of Zion: 'You are my people an' I will put my words in your mout' an' hide you in de SHADOW of my han''. Awake! put on de strengt' of de Lord! LOOSE de bonds of sin an' unrighteousness from off your neck. If dy tongue offend dee PLUCK it out: if dy eye offend dee PLUCK it out. Otherwise de fires of HELL will burn in your heart.

Not because you feel you young and strong mean you must be too proud to come to de Lord. Remember Samson, the son of Manoah? He born to save his people, but because he was proud he listen to de voice of de Devil an' dey blin' him and brought him low. De Lord is callin' you tonight to leave your sinful ways an' follow Him who is de Way de Truth an' de Light. Harken to His commandments an' your peace will be wide an' deep as de river Jordan self. He will CLEAVE de rock an' de waters of life will flow an' de land bring fort' honey an' milk. Fear not, set de Lord, for I am your God. [*The hymn 'Whoseover will' is again started by a solitary female voice, joined by tambourine and then by other singers, some of whom clap in time to the music. The leader, who had occasionally added his own comments, like 'Tell them, sister'; 'Praise the Lord'; 'Halleluia', etc. as footnotes during the previous speech; now, with one hand, flips the pages of the Bible and chooses his text. A more articulate speaker, he commands respect with an apocalyptic style of delivery, almost hypnotic use of hand and eye – tightly controlled – reminiscent of the static dynamism of the Stanley Greaves painting:* THE PREACHER]

PREACHER And I heard a loud voice in Heaven saying: 'Now is come salvation and strength, and the kingdom of our God. Fret not thyself because of evildoers, neither be thou envious against the workers of iniquity. For they shall soon be cut DOWN like the grass an' WITHER as the green leaf. TRUST in the Lord and do good.' Trust in the Lord. . . . It say TRUST! Trust mean to BELIEVE in God, and it is something that must come from deep down inside you. It's only when you put all your FAITH in the Lord Jehovah that you will find that He is your rock

and foundation. Otherwise is build you building on
shifting sand. You see how when the thunder and
lightning start how the rain and the wind does blow
down even big Samaan trees – some of them more
than a hundred years old – as if they was
matchsticks? But even though the tree is big and have
many branches, the roots-them [*Pronounced as one
word*] don't go deep. They FOUNDATION is shallow. Is
just so those who are weak in they FAITH, though they
might talk big, unless they root DEEP in the Lord the
winds of unrighteousness and sin will blow them down
like STRAW! Remember the dream of King
Nebuchadnezzar. Lying in bed dreaming, a vision came
to him – a powerful statue with a head make out of gold
and the body of silver and brass – yet when a little
stone only touch it so . . . it mash up in little pieces.
Because, the feet, my friends, the FEET was made of
CLAY. The FOUNDATIONS was not strong in the LORD.
Yes, and even though he was a mighty king, when he
turn his face from the Lord God Jehovah the Devil
enter his soul and this KING start to eat grass like a
BEAST and the hair of his body come like feathers and
his nails all turn to CLAWS. And he was sore afraid. Now
they have few people today very well who, like
Nebuchadnezzar, when they see how sin turning them
ugly – they get afraid. But 'Fear not,' seth the Lord, 'I
am the first and the last. I am he that liveth and was
dead and behold I am alive and have the keys of life
and death.'

Brothers and sisters, today we seeing how the scriptures
coming true. The powers of darkness busy in the land.
Today the world standing at the crossroads. [*Traces a
cross on the ground with staff*] The people of Zion have
loss their way. Rouse yourself in the Lord! 'Behold!' seth
the Lord. 'I lift up my HAND to the nations and RAISE
my signal to the peoples. Go forth from this
BABYLON . . . BACK to the Holy Land and the sacred
river Jordan. Fear not for I am with you. Behold your
God will come with VENGEANCE. The LION of Judah
will SCATTER your enemies. Then shall the deaf hear
and the eyes of the BLIND be opened.' Isaiah, Chapter 35.

But hear me, the Lord say, hear me. You will have to
BORN again. 'For whosoever save his life shall lose it,
and whosoever lose his life for my sake shall have life
everlasting.' Brothers and Sisters, these are the words
of the Book of Books. Except a man be born again he
cannot see the kingdom of God. Except a man SUFFER
and be born of water AND the spirit, he cannot enter
into the kingdom of God, who is the Lord of the
living and the dead. This life is full of pain and
suffering. But is out of SUFFERING cometh salvation.
I am the door. By me if any enter, he shall be saved.
If any man have ears to hear let him hear. Allelulia.
Salvation and Glory and Honour and POWER unto the
Lord God Jehovah. Give us a hymn there, sister!
[*The hymn 'You must be born again' starts up. An
uninhibited, syncopated, totally convincing performance
towards the end of which the light dims, goes out, leaving
only the lighted candles on the table. The group pick up
their possessions – the* PRIEST *and the* BOY *carry the table
and the women bear the lighted candles – and* EXIT.]

Scene Ten

Night. LIONEL'S *studio. He is painting feverishly – adding touches to a
fantastic canvas: the figure of a Composite Man, something like an
Aztec/Toltec totem, made up of African/Amerindian/Hindu elements.
A half human, half animal/bird thing which is grotesque. The* ROBE
*painting, among others, is prominently displayed. He steps back, puts
palette and brushes* [*one of them held between teeth*] *on table, looking
fixedly at work all the time, wiping hands on an oil-stained rag.
Apparently not pleased with the work, he throws rag on table and
collapses in chair c.s., eyes closed in fatigue.*

PAT [*Off*] Lionel! Lionel!

LIONEL [*Wearily, almost to himself*] Yes.

PAT Lionel! Your food is getting cold! You not coming up?

LIONEL [*Loudly*] Yes! I'm coming just now.
[*Gets up after a while and goes over to* ROBE *painting.
Stands before it for a few seconds and then abruptly*

picks it up and puts it, after looking around room, on the central chair. He stands away from it, looking at it, as PAT *enters.*]

PAT [*She has brought his dinner on a tray.*] I decided to bring your dinner down. If I worry to wait till you come upstairs to eat it it would spoil. [*He takes the tray and places it on the crowded table.*]

LIONEL Thanks, Pat. You shouldn't have bothered ...

PAT Well, if Mohammed won't come to the mountain, the mountain will come to him. Li, this painting is so important that you have to stop eating even? [*He has taken up the plate and is toying with the food.*]

LIONEL I just don't feel hungry, that's all. Too much on my mind. Too much to DO, Pat. [*He prongs a piece of meat on the word 'do' – action suggesting frustration. She looks at the* ROBE *painting.*]

PAT And you can do what you have to do by starving yourself? And by not looking after your health? [*Indicates the half-empty bottle on table*] Rum can't take the place of food, you know.

LIONEL [*Between deliberate mouthfuls*] Look, Pat. You don't understand. I can't really explain it, but this exhibition ... well, it's [*A strange tone creeps into his voice – an earnestness*] something that I HAVE to do – and soon. There isn't TIME.

PAT Lionel, you mind if I sit in that chair? My feet are killing me.

LIONEL Oh, let me move this [*Puts painting on floor against foot of easel*]

PAT [*Sitting*] Thanks. How you mean you haven't got time? Nobody set a date when the paintings have to be finished.

LIONEL I know. But it isn't just the exhibition. It's me. I HAVE to finish them. [*He has put down plate and now goes up to easel*] You see this? What does it look like to you? An abstract painting? What Arthur calls 'surrealistic

47

	fantasy'? You want me to tell you what it is? It's not an abstract painting [*He is now apparently oblivious of her presence*]. It's a vision. A dream. You think dreams aren't real? They are, Pat. They are. [*Turning to her suddenly*] But this. This is a fake. [*Indicates painting.*] It's a fake because it's not complete. It's not whole. And it isn't whole because . . . because . . . [*He has to put his hand over his eyes as if dizzy*]
PAT	[*Leaning forward, alarmed*] Lionel? LI? What's wrong?
LIONEL	[*Turning to her. Suddenly O.K. again*] It's all right. It's nothing. Headache.
PAT	Lionel. Why you don't take a rest from the painting? Just for a couple days.
LIONEL	I CAN'T. Don't you SEE? I have to try and get them down. The ideas and images in my head. Before they fade again. [*He points to paintings*] You see? They're not finished. Not one of them. [*He goes to her, dropping down by her knees to speak straight to her. He is feverishly earnest.*] Pat. I feel as if . . . as if just a LITTLE longer, just a little bit longer, and I'll be able to do it. Then the vision will take shape. Become whole. You remember Arthur said once that a robe was meant to be worn? Now I know what he meant. Even though he himself didn't. I can FEEL there's a door in my mind that won't open: the door between dream and reality: living and dead: between past and present. And I have got to open that door and walk through it!
PAT	[*While he has been speaking she has seen him only as a mother sees an earnest, wrong-headed child: in need of both censure and protection. Now she is genuinely alarmed.*] Lionel. You mustn't talk like that. Please, PLEASE! [*She cups his face in her hands.*] You MUST take a break from your work. You NEED the rest. Look how thin you're getting. You can't teach all day and work all night. Leave the painting and come to bed.
LIONEL	[*Getting up abruptly*] I CAN'T, Pat. . . .
PAT	[*With the anger of desperation*] You mean you WON'T!

	[*Getting up to go*] You're just being selfish! Only thinking of yourself and what YOU want. Well, if you want to go blind and kill yourself with your precious painting go right ahead. Don't think about me or about the baby! [*She starts to leave.*]
LIONEL	You won't even TRY to understand. You won't even TRY!
PAT	[*Turning like a wounded animal*] TRY TO UNDERSTAND WHAT? All I see is that you're killing yourself with all this damn stupidness and this crazy talk about visions!
LIONEL	[*With calm, almost desolate anger*] Stupidness . . .? Crazy talk . . .? Yes. That's what you think, isn't it? You and everybody else. That's what you REALLY think.
PAT	[*She is immediately contrite, suddenly aware of the damage.*] Lionel, I'm sorry. I didn't really . . . [*Comes up to him. He turns away.*] Oh Lionel, don't behave like a child. I didn't mean to . . . [*Puts out a hand to touch him.*]
LIONEL	Don't touch me. DON'T TOUCH ME!
PAT	[*Takes his arm as if to turn him towards her. He throws it off viciously – she gasps – he goes to hammock.*] But Lionel, you're being a . . .
LIONEL	Leave me alone. [*Sits in hammock.* PAT *takes a step towards him. He gets right in and pulls the sides over himself so that he is completely enclosed.*] JUST GO AWAY AND LEAVE ME ALONE! [*This from inside hammock.* PAT, *who is now on the point of tears, stands helplessly over the hammock for a few moments, then goes quickly.*]

Scene Eleven

As lights dim and fade to blackout, bring up forest sounds and hold as music begins. Sound of Chinese chime-bells shaken lightly followed, one after another, by gourd-rattle, drum, bamboo horn and finally, flute melody. Volume of sound should increase gradually as instruments added until all are playing together. At the point at which the flute melody is heard a spot picks up s.r. a figure – a human totem made up of three dancers; the lowest [squatting] in Arawak, the middle [half stooping] in West African, and the topmost in Southern Indian ritual costume. The 'totem' moves its arms in a gentle, undulating rhythm – a suggestion of Shiva, the creator/destroyer – there is a new sound, a rhythmic, bell-like sound, as Carib dancers [naked except for lion-cloths the strings of which pass between the buttocks giving the impression of total nudity from behind] enter wearing anklets made of rows of small harness-bells. Their movements – a slow shuffling, stamping dance, arms hanging loosely as they crouch and swing – are designed to create the impression of a circle continually broken and re-formed. Each of the three dancers who make up the totem takes a turn within the centre of the ring, each using movements which suggest the aspect of the totem which he represents. The total effect is of a MANDALA *– an effect heightened perhaps by use of lighting to throw a circular, centrifugal pattern on the stage. The masque reaches a climax during which coloured streamers, torches or flares etc. are carried by the dancers, thrown into the air etc. to the increasingly insistent rhythm of drum, ankle-bells and horns. Abruptly, at a given signal [cymbals?] the music and dancing stop as the* ASHANTI PRIEST *and* ARAWAK SHAMAN *enter, masked, from opposite sides d.s. centre eventually standing close together facing audience. The dancers move forward d.s. separating into two 'ranks' on either side of c.s. where, on a platform, the figure of the* DREAMER *is gradually flooded by an overhead spot so that he appears to be caught inside an inverted cone of light. All turn towards him, and as he rises [unmasked: it is Lionel] and descends coming towards the priest and shaman who wait to receive him, the dancers move apart to let him pass, closing ranks behind him. They now begin a movement which results in a steady rhythm of ankle-bells.* LIONEL *is now facing* PRIEST *and* SHAMAN. *The* PRIEST *steps forward.*

PRIEST   The door of spirits has opened. He who was dead has risen up. Great Ta Kora river of life that flows from the rock: Asase Ya, tree of mother and child where our people began, in whose branches the tiger rests, beneath whose roots our ancestors sleep; receive this son of Tano [*Each time he speaks he holds out a bowl into which* LIONEL [*as if in a dream*] *dips a finger.*] White. For milk, whose spirit is air.
Black. For water, whose womb is earth.

Red. For blood, whose heart is fire.
[*As he steps back,* SHAMAN *comes forward. As he speaks a gigantic replica of the* ROBE *painting – made of cloth – descends from the ceiling, behind* LIONEL.]

SHAMAN Receive, Couvade, this robe of the sun. Great Earthmaker look kindly on our people. Let no flame burn them, water drown them. Protector of animals, birds and fishes, do not let harm come to our crops; fruit of the land, milk of the land. Receive this son of Makanater, O lord of living and dead. [*The* ROBE *is behind* LIONEL *now, at floor level. He backs into it and it is released, falling to cover him. On the outside there is an ornate silver and gold sun – a flaming disc. The dancers have been increasing the tempo of the bells and now all raise their arms heavenwards, fingers outspread, as music returns. This time with an added, electronic whine rising in pitch and volume as dancers chant 'Dendé, dendé, dendé'. The* ROBE *is removed from* LIONEL *and he emerges, covered in blood, which runs down his outstretched arms. In the midst of all this we hear* LIONEL'S *scream: a hideous cry of anguish, his hands clawing at his face, pulling the thick paint down in streaks, like blood. As he falls to his knees, head upraised like a sacrificial bull, the music, bells, etc. stop. He is caught immobile for a second or two in the light. Brief blackout. Lights come up to reveal* LIONEL *lying alone on stage, his face streaked with paint.* PAT *enters in nightgown – frantic.*]

PAT Lionel! Lionel!
[*Sees him on floor. She drops to her knees as her mouth opens in a silent scream of pain.*]

BLACKOUT

Part Four

The Child of the Vessel

Scene Twelve

Brilliant morning. LIONEL'S *house.* PAT *in nightgown, sitting up in bed. Outside, the sounds of the street.* EDDIE *knocks, enters, pushing door open wide with one foot. He is carrying a tray with coffee, etc. His shirt unbuttoned and not tucked in.*

EDDIE Well how's the patient? Still alive? Breakfast-time!

PAT But look at this man! Eddie, you really shouldn't, I told you not to bother. I'm not bed-ridden, you know.

EDDIE [*Mimics radio announcer's faked breeziness*] This is the Eddie Richards' Breakfast Special! Hot orange juice, cold coffee, smashed eggs AND burnt toast. Just for you. [*Resumes normal voice*] How you feeling? [*Places tray on bedside table, sits on bed and arranges pillows as backrest.*]

PAT [*Amused in spite of herself*] A lot better, thanks.

EDDIE Girl you must be. You were up this morning before ME. I heard you moving around up here. Or you didn't sleep too well?

PAT Well, no, I didn't. Sorry if I woke you . . .

EDDIE Me? You know me. Sleep like a log. Naw. I was awake. Just too lazy to get up.

PAT [*Sipping coffee*] Who said it's cold? It's fine. Just right. Your breakfast special looks very nice. [*Nibbling toast*] So that's what you were so busy doing in the kitchen! You had something already?

EDDIE Only coffee. I can't eat in the morning. My stomach don't wake up till about half past twelve. [*Gets up and*

	goes over to dressing table, buttoning up shirt] Lionel has a great set-up down there, man. I see he's even put in sink and toilet!
PAT	[*Subdued*] Yes. He was LIVING in that studio of his. You should have slept in the small bedroom, Eddie. Down there smells of paint.
EDDIE	[*Brushing hair*] It would take more than the smell of paint to stop me from sleeping, girl. Anyway, if I'd slept up here my snoring would have kept you awake. By the way, when the doctor coming again? Today?
PAT	Yes. This afternoon.
EDDIE	[*Coming across to her, brush in hand, points to a bottle of clear yellowish liquid*] And that's the medicine you have to take? [*Picks it up from bedside table*] You want to know what it looks like? [*Laughs*]
PAT	[*Making a face*] I know. It tastes horrible. The thing makes me feel sleepy and stupidy the whole day.
EDDIE	[*Replacing bottle, takes a final look in mirror, puts brush on dressing table*] Well, you need to keep yourself quiet. That fall on the steps could have made a whole lot o'trouble, hear?
PAT	[*Dully*] Yes. I know.
EDDIE	[*Lights a cigarette, then turns chair round and sits, arms resting on back of it*] Pat. What really happen night before last? But if you prefer not to . . .
PAT	No. it's all right, Eddie. But you know already. As much as I do, anyway. All I know is I heard him scream out, and by the time I got downstairs there he was lying on the floor with the place in darkness. I thought . . . Eddie, I thought he was dead . . .
EDDIE	It must have been a hell of a shock for you. But you're a real worrier, you know. People don't just die so.
PAT	Anyway, it's a good thing you came when you did.

53

EDDIE I didn't know WHAT to do. All I could think of was to bundle both of you into the car and drive straight to the hospital. I don't know which one of the three of us was the most frightened. . . . Lionel look like a ghost, you were crying out with pain . . . or fright . . .

PAT Both.

EDDIE . . . and I was scared like hell, I tell you. I thought you were going to have the baby right there and then.

PAT Lord, if you hadn't come . . .

EDDIE Well, anyway that's all over now. How much longer they keeping Lionel in that hospital?

PAT Only a few more days, I hope. It's the anaemia. He had a bad case of it, they said. They're giving him four injections a day, and he has to have more drops in his eyes.

EDDIE They love giving injections there. They must be a bunch of witch doctors in that damn hospital, the way they like sticking needles into people.

PAT Eddie, you'll go and see him today? This afternoon?

EDDIE Sure. After work.

PAT Just to keep him company for a bit.

EDDIE I'll go and see him Pat, don't worry. I got to take home a few groceries and so on for the old man, but I'll drop in at the hospital afterwards.

PAT Poor Eddie. We really have you running up and down eh?

EDDIE [*With exaggerated weariness*] Ow, yes chile. Between you, Lionel and the old man you-all have me like a yo-yo. [*Getting up to remove tray*] Finished with this?

PAT Yes. Thanks. Just leave everything in the sink, Eddie. [*He goes off*]

EDDIE [*Off*] By the way. Arthur said he was going to visit Lionel today.

PAT   Good. I'm glad. You know, I feel a bit guilty about Arthur.

EDDIE   [*Off*] Guilty? About what?

PAT   I never liked him. But he's been a good friend to Lionel. [*Eddie reappears*] Eddie, the way he went and spoke to the principal. Even fixed up for sick leave for Lionel. He didn't have to do that.

EDDIE   Old Arthur is all right. He has a good heart. These days since he's a big party member and ting making platform speeches, you know. Man! He's really smelling himself! I hope he don't start talking politics when he goes to visit Lionel. It's good thing he wasn't there when Lionel was saying . . . you know, when we were in the car.

PAT   [*Apprehensive*] You understood what he was saying?

EDDIE   Well. He wasn't exactly sober, you know. Funny. That's the first time I've ever seen your husband drunk. He was saying something about a game and a stone . . . and oh! yes. 'Arthur's game is the way of the trickster.' I wonder what Arthur would have thought about that.

PAT   But the way he looked at us! Eddie, it was as if we weren't there. He couldn't have had so much to drink . . .

EDDIE   Pat, Lionel had been drinking on an empty stomach, right? And he was a sick man besides. Burning up with fever. What you expect?

PAT   But what about all those queer dreams he was having? And that scream? . . .

EDDIE   You ready to start imagining all kinds of terrible things wrong with him, eh? They examined Lionel from head to foot at the hospital. They said it was . . . I forget the name they called it. Not enough blood in the brain. Anyway, it's that caused the collapse. Look, this anaemia is a hell of a thing, hear? His blood must have been as thin as water.

PAT   There's something I didn't tell you, Eddie. His face.
When I found him it was all covered in paint. I
cleaned it off. [*Having confessed, she looks to him for
an explanation, hopefully*]

EDDIE   Paint? He fell on the paint, or what? What happened?

PAT   No. It wasn't the fall. The paint on his face was . . .
like stripes. Black and red and white stripes all down
his face [*She is upset*] . . . Like if they were painted on.
It was horrible, Eddie.

EDDIE   You mean he did it himself? Christ! He must have
been drunk as a fish.

PAT   I don't think he was drunk. I believe it was some sort
of mental breakdown he had . . .

EDDIE   [*Trying to reassure her*] But they examined him and
they didn't . . .

PAT   They didn't see his face how it looked! You were
there. You heard the things he was saying. He was like
a stranger. Somebody we didn't know at all. And you
yourself said how when you saw him yesterday how
strange he was – as if he didn't recognise you! [*She is
overwrought now.*] Oh Eddie, [*Leaning towards him*]
suppose he's still like that when the baby comes? [*She
suddenly straightens, arches her back, with a cry,
holding her side.*]

EDDIE   [*Helping her back against pillows*] Take it easy now,
Pat. Take it easy. Listen, it's not Lionel who's having
this baby. It's you. You'll have enough to think about.
Don't worry about Lionel. With all those vitamins
they're shooting into him he'll be a new man in no
time at all. [*She begins to relax. Closes her eyes.*] O.K.?
Pain gone now? [*She nods.*] Jesus! Don't scare me like
that again, hear? [*Reaches across and picks up bottle of
medicine*] When you suppose to take the first dose of
this horse pee?

PAT   Now. A tablespoon.

EDDIE   [*Picks up spoon from same table*] This is a tablespoon?

	[*She nods*] O.K. Open up. [*Administers medicine. She swallows, makes a wry face*]
PAT	Ugh. It's AWFUL!
EDDIE	[*Sniffs medicine, then looks at it malevolently*] Bloody witch doctors! [*Replaces it and gets up.*] Well, I better make a move if I'm to get to'work in time this morning. How you feeling now? O.K.? [*She nods.*]
PAT	Coming back for lunch?
EDDIE	Uh huh. But I just hope that this woman who supposed to be looking after you and doing the cooking [*Looks at his watch*] – she's late again, by the way – I hope she's not poisoning us. [*He is at the door.*]
PAT	Oh Eddie. The lady's cooking isn't so bad.
EDDIE	Not so bad? She's a worse cook than me! That fried rice she did yesterday was like dry ochroe seeds. The same colour and all.
PAT	[*Laughing*] You better don't let her hear you, or she will poison you in truth.
EDDIE	Anyway. I'll see you later, eh?
PAT	O.K. Eddie. [*He leaves.*]
	Dim out as she turns her head, her face suddenly sad, serious again.

Scene Thirteen

Mid-morning. LIONEL'S *room in hospital. Single chair, small table, vase of sunflowers.* LIONEL *sitting up in hospital bed, knees drawn up under blanket. He wears ill-fitting, baggy hospital pyjamas. His eyes are thickly bandaged. Over the bed a mosquito net hangs white, ominous.* ARTHUR *seated in chair.*

ARTHUR	. . . And you have to keep that thing on all the time?
LIONEL	In the day. When they put the drops in.
ARTHUR	But you'll be out in a couple of days' time, so it's not so bad, eh?

LIONEL   [*Dully, withdrawn*] So they tell me.

ARTHUR   Well. How are they treating you? That nurse who was here just now – SHE'S a sweet little thing, boy! – I hope she's . . . ah, looking after you nicely, you know. [LIONEL *nods.*] Man! I envy you. [*No response*] Although I must say I don't envy those injections! [*Trying hard to salvage the conversation*] Eddie says you're so full of punctures now, that you have to be careful how you drink water. [*Laughs*] That brother-in-law of yours is a real clown, you know.

LIONEL   [*With a ghost of a smile*] Yes. A clown. Not like me. I'm just a scarecrow.

ARTHUR   Scarecrow? Come now, man. You've lost weight, but not all that much.

LIONEL   Pat says I'm just skin and bones. Look [*Spreads his arms laterally, hands hanging down from slack wrists – like a scarecrow's arms in their baggy sleeves*] – a scarecrow. [*He retracts his arms. The same curiously detached, automatic movement.*]

ARTHUR   [*Uncomfortably*] Well if you ask me, it's those hospital pyjamas. They're miles too big for you. Makes you look like some half-starved prisoner.

LIONEL   [*With deadly seriousness*] Oh no. They feed me very well. But you see that? [*Indicates the net overhead*] Mosquitoes are trapped up there. In that net. Every night they feed on me. Suck my blood.

ARTHUR   [*Not sure whether* LIONEL *has made a joke or not*] Why you don't get the nurse to kill them? [*Gets up to investigate net*] I don't see any. [*Taps net.*] Maybe they escaped. Bet the net has big holes in it. Hospital stuff, boy. [*Taps net*] No mosquitoes in there.

LIONEL   [*Without looking up*] You won't see them during the day. But at night I can hear them buzzing in my ears. They're there all right. [ARTHUR *taps net again causing the whole thing to spin gently.*] So you're a busy busy politician nowadays. [LIONEL *says this in the same flat voice, again without looking up.*]

ARTHUR [*Stops net spinning round. Looks down at* LIONEL, *surprised at sudden turn in conversation.*] Me? [*Laughs*] No, man not really. I do some work for the party: mainly book-keeping. [*Sits*] I've only spoken at one meeting so far; but, boy, that was an experience!

LIONEL Game of the trickster. A dangerous game.

ARTHUR Politics? Well [*Sensing thin ice*] it depends. . . . Only if you try to fool the people. It's like all power. It depends how you use it.

LIONEL The game of the stone.

ARTHUR [*Puzzled, but playing it by ear*] What? . . . Oh . . . you mean that terrible business about old John Buckman? [*Takes out a cigarette from a silver case*] That was a nasty affair. They say he may never be able to walk again. The blow damaged some part of the brain. [*Puts cigarette between lips, then suddenly takes it out*] Oh, Lionel. It's all right to smoke. . . ?

LIONEL Yes, go ahead.

ARTHUR [*Lighting up, exhaling luxuriously*] Yes. That was a hell of a thing. According to the P.N.P. it was a deliberate attack against them. To put them out of the running. But that is a load of rubbish. Everybody knows Buckman got most of his money and a lot of his property from some very shady deals. You can bet it was some private grudge a couple of his 'friends' were settling up with him.

ARTHUR Anyway it looks as if the P.N.P. are using the incident to get votes. Especially in the rural areas. Buckman was from Manoa, you know; and they're a clannish lot up there. They never liked the government anyway.

LIONEL [*Suddenly turning pointedly towards him*] Arthur. Tell me, do you ever dream?

ARTHUR [*Caught unawares*] Dream? Well . . . yes. Of course. Sometimes. I mean . . . well, everybody dreams.

LIONEL   But not everybody listens to their dreams. [*An awkward pause*] You know what happens when I dream?

ARTHUR   [*Extremely uncomfortable*] No, no, tell me about it.

LIONEL   In the darkness, music comes. Like little bells. I can hear my heart beating. I'm shaking like a leaf and I can't stop myself. I'm in a forest. It's dark. Very dark. Now I'm getting smaller and smaller; and the things around me start to grow. Rocks grow into mountains, trees seem to be growing right up into the stars ... I'm like a child, a little child. I can see all kinds of things: huge birds and animals, images, idols. There is a river nearby. I can hear the water running, singing, like the trees and the stars. I dip my hands into the black water, to drink, but when I lift my hands up they're empty. Then the dances begin. [*He seems to have come to the end of his speech.*]

ARTHUR   [*Out of his depth, but trying to keep contact*] And then what happens?

LIONEL   [*Leaning towards him earnestly*] I must learn the dances. Not for myself, you see. For the others. I have to teach them the dances. Teach them what I learn. Do you understand? All things are part of one wholeness. One mandala.

ARTHUR   I see.

LIONEL   Do you? Arthur? Do you SEE?

ARTHUR   [*Confused and embarrassed*] Well I ... I don't know very much about these things ... [*Suddenly, clutching at straws*] Wait! What about using these ideas in your painting? These ... dreams are perfect abstract images ... like a dance ...

LIONEL   [*With quiet finality*] No. The dances are real. Art is the illusion.

ARTHUR   But Lionel, these are great ideas. You ought to use them. You haven't forgotten about your exhibition, I hope.

LIONEL [*His manner is reverting to its original passivity.*] You said once that a robe is meant to be worn, remember?

ARTHUR Oh, you mean that painting about ancestors. . . . Well, we both said a lot of things that day . . .

LIONEL [*Almost wearily*] You were right. Only you didn't know. . . . There was something you didn't understand.

ARTHUR How do you mean?

LIONEL To wear it you have to be born again. [*He has withdrawn into himself now.*]

ARTHUR [*Seeing his cue*] Christ! Look at the time! [*Checking his watch*] Lionel, boy I've got to run. [*Stubs out cigarette*] I'll be late getting back to work. [*Gets up*] Look, I'll see you tomorrow, eh? [*No response. He stands there undecided.*] Oh, I dropped in to see Pat yesterday. She's fine.

LIONEL Yes. She bears the child of the vessel. [*This in an emotionless voice.*]

ARTHUR [*Voice and manner convey a baffled, sincere regret.*] Yes. Well, I'll see you, Lionel. [*Exit*]

Dim out as LIONEL *raises head slowly towards net overhead.*

Scene Fourteen

In this scene lighting is used to pick out, in succession and as accurately as possible, three areas of the stage where characters speak [within their own 'space' as it were] and move before they freeze – held static in their own area – while other areas are lit and animated, they too, in their turn, becoming static, contained spaces; the whole thing to resemble the discontinuous, outlined figures one associates with an early Greaves painting.
On a darkened stage a telephone rings. Spot comes up on chair and small table with phone. ARTHUR, *breathless and sweating, hurries on and answers it. As he speaks he makes himself more comfortable by unbuttoning* [*unlacing?*] *his shirt, finally taking it off.*

ARTHUR   Hello. Hi, Eddie. I'm glad you rang . . . Naw, boy.
           Just back from work. You heard the news? . . . How
           you mean what news? Came over the radio this mid-
           day. Trouble in the interior! . . . what? . . . no. Man.
           Real trouble. Soldiers being flown up there . . . to
           Manoa . . . YES!! People getting shot and killed, I
           tell you! . . . How it started? A couple of young
           criminals attacked a P.N.P. man with a stone. To settle
           an old debt. . . . Yes. Old Buckman that died in
           hospital the other day . . . yes, man. Eddie, what the
           ass is wrong with you? You don't read the papers or
           what? . . . You're telling me? The whole thing blowing
           up now like a revolution. And general elections only a
           week off . . . eh? . . . yes . . . that's right. The P.N.P.
           They started fanning the fire and now only Christ
           knows where it will all end. The whole place buzzing
           with the news, man. Where've you been? . . . Oh. . . .
           How is he? . . . You see what I told you? . . . right!
           Just as if he's somewhere else . . . yes . . . yes . . . well,
           that's the usual procedure . . . yes . . . it's so he's under
           observation, that's all. You haven't told Pat. . . . No
           . . . right! If she saw him like that. . . . Absolutely!
           Christ, everything's in a mess. And the baby is due
           any time now? . . . At home? But look, Eddie, you
           don't think it would be better if she had it at the
           maternity centre. . . ? O.K. chief. Just an idea. I
           suppose you-all know what you're doing. Maybe
           you're right. Look, Eddie, give me a ring as soon as
           things develop, eh? . . . yes. . . . No, no. I won't say
           anything . . . right. See you. [*Replaces phone, remains
           seated, thoughtful. Freeze as spot dims.*]

Second spot comes up on PAT *lying in bed. She is in early labour.*
EDDIE *seated at bedside. Two women: midwife and assistant stand
by. One busy with basin and towel, sponging* PAT'S *face: the other
waits, frostily polite, for* EDDIE *to leave.*

PAT   [*Forlorn, near to tears*] But why, Eddie? Why they
           haven't let him come out of hospital yet?

EDDIE   They can't discharge him yet, Pat. He's still very weak.
           He asked me to tell you how sorry he is he can't be

	here with you. He really feels bad about it, Pat. But they think he can come home tomorrow. I'm sure he'll be here tomorrow.
PAT	But I want him now. The baby's coming and I need him. I'm frightened, Eddie.
EDDIE	[*Looking helplessly at midwife who looks pointedly at her watch*] Take it easy, Pat. And don't worry. Your job now is to have this baby. Think how happy you're going to make Lionel. The baby means a lot to him, you know. To him it's another little Lionel you're having. So you have a big job to do, hear? But there's nothing to worry about. [*She moans as she gets a pain, the midwife motions him to leave.*] I have to go now, Pat. I'll be waiting downstairs. Don't worry. Everything's going to be all right.
PAT	Eddie, Eddie. Get Lionel. Please. I want Lionel. [*She is in tears.*]

They freeze as he takes her hand. Spot dims. Third spot comes up on LIONEL *as we saw him last. Ward nurse enters with tray, metal pan, etc.*

NURSE	[*With bustling, genial, superficial good humour*] Time for your injection, Teach. [*Rests tray on table,* LIONEL *sits immobile, absent*]
NURSE	Wait. You still not talking to me? You frien'? [*Business with syringe, needle, etc.*] Ow me goy. Is what I do you? I not you frien' any more, then? [*Shrugs, undisturbed by his silence*] Anyhow, you KNOW I have to give you your injection. [*Prepares a cotton swab and stands, syringe in one hand, swab in the other, poised but undecided*] Is which arm it is this time? [*Lionel sticks out an arm, the hand hanging loosely. Nurse deftly pushes his sleeve up with syringe hand, applies swab with the other hand, then gives the injection. A casual, virtuoso performance*] So you not speaking to me no more. All right, then. But I sorry. [*Putting things back in dish. She is in constant movement as she speaks. Nurse removes bandage from his eyes.*] You're an important patient now, you know, Teach.

Tomorrow mornin' is two doctors coming here. Chief consultant and specialist. Both of them comin' just to see you. So you see how you lucky? Not one, but two doctors. [*Begins putting net down.*] Tonight you have to get an early night, so you wake up bright and early. Like a new man. [*Tucking in net.*] What you say? I'm going to turn off the light now. [*Pauses at the door.*] O.K.? Goodnight, Teach. [*Light goes off as she switches it off. Exit. Directly above the* [*open*] *top of the net a small spot comes up slowly, so that* LIONEL *is seen caught within an inverted cone of light inside the mosquito net. He squats on the bed, having assumed just before the lights came up, the* DREAMER'S *'foetal' position. His eyes are open.*]

There are now three areas of light – three tableaux – on the stage. These are now extinguished one by one. ARTHUR'S *spot fades, followed by* PAT'S *and* EDDIE'S *and after a few seconds' pause,* LIONEL'S *light fades very gradually to:*

BLACKOUT

The rainforest.
In the darkness the sound of chinese chime bells. After a few seconds Black Carib song [*as in opening of play*] *comes up as spot c.s. gradually brightens over a baby's cot with netting down. Dimly-lit figures of Carib dancers, etc. come on silently to squat in a semicircle just out of spotlit area with central cot.*
SHAMAN *and* PRIEST [*unmasked*] *come on from opposite sides and stand d.s. to left and right of crib. Singing stops. From now on, the only musical sound is that of chime-bells. The* ASHANTI PRIEST *begins the final invocation: He speaks with a sense of the occasion, but also with the simplicity of deep emotion and sincere belief.*

PRIEST   Now the edges of the years have met. The path and the stream are one. Great Ta Kora, spirit of our ancestors, supreme being upon whom men lean and do not fall, from whose rock the sacred Tano flows, make our people strong. We call upon you in darkness; we call upon you in sunlight. Let no evil thing come to this child. Let no harm come to this child, when the sun rises in the morning, when the cock crows in the early dawn. Give life to the head of our people; life to

our women; life to our men; life to our children.
These words are a voice from the mouth of us all. We
are addressing you, O Tano, and you will understand:
[*Turns to the crib*] Sleep, Couvade, and dream our
dream. [*Steps back into the shadows*]

SHAMAN [*Coming forward in his turn*]
We, your children ask you, O Makanater, Great
Earthmaker
whose face is the mountain
whose eye is the sun
whose hair is the forest;
We ask you to receive this dust of manioc [*Extends arm to let the powder fall from his hand, between the fingers*]
Milk of the calabash
Fruit of the land
which comes from our heart.
We speak from our heart.
[*Lights come up to reveal* LIONEL, ARTHUR, EDDIE *and* PAT *standing on small platforms u.s., behind and above the line of dancers, etc.*]
Receive us, Great Earthmaker.
Those who are suffering
Those who are tired
Those who have sickness
Those who have pain
In their lowly body
In their lowly mind
Who cannot see your goodness
For this we are stooping low
beside you
before you
beneath you.
Receive us, O Makanater,
Receive us, lord of the forests
So we may walk in your eye
So we walk in your heart. [*Gestures towards crib*]
Sleep, Couvade, and dream our dream.

As backstage lights begin to fade, dancers, etc. all chant softly:
'Dendé, dendé, dendé, uamánia' [*Twice*] *Finally, the spot over the crib fades gradually to blackout. The chime-bells stop.*

FINIS

Michael Gilkes,
Photograph Anna Rutherford

Michael Gilkes has workéd for over twenty years in Caribbean Theatre as actor, director/dramaturge- and playwright. He is the author of five plays: *Young Assop* (a play for children) *Intransit*, *This Island Now*, *A Pleasant Career* (a play about the life and fiction af Edgar Mittelholzer) and *Couvade*.

Couvade (first published in 1974) is his first published play. It was inspired by the work of Wilson Harris, and has been performed in the Caribbean, Great Britain and Africa.

Michael Gilkes is, at present, Reader in British and Caribbean literature and Head of the Department of English at the U.W.I. campus in Barbados.